The
QUILTS
of the
BRITISH
ISLES

The
QUILTS
of the
BRITISH
ISLES

Janet Rae

Photographs by David Cripps

E. P. DUTTON ⟁ NEW YORK

Published in the United States by E. P. Dutton,
a division of NAL Penguin Inc.,
2 Park Avenue, New York, N.Y. 10016.

Designed and produced by
Bellew Publishing Company Limited
7 Southampton Place, London WC1A 2DR

Library of Congress Catalog Card Number: 87-70958

ISBN: 0-525-24573-1 (cloth)

ISBN: 0-525-48341-1 (DP)

10 9 8 7 6 5 4 3 2 1

First American Edition

Printed and bound in Spain by Graficromo, S.A.

Frontispiece: Pieced cotton scrap quilt with brown print
border backed with white cotton. Made as a wedding quilt by
Annie Heslop of Durham about 1825 and handed down
within the family. The quilting designs follow the block
pattern of the piecing, and a lovers' knot has been quilted in
the centre. 8 ft 5 in × 8 ft 9 in (257 cm × 267 cm). (Beamish
North of England Open Air Museum)

Contents

Preface

The current enthusiasm for patchwork, quilting and appliqué – all the needlework techniques used by the modern quiltmaker – has fostered interest in the heritage of this craft in Britain. Inevitably, comparisons have been drawn with the development of quiltmaking in the United States. When I began looking in earnest at antique British quilts over six years ago, I soon realized that such comparisons could be misleading; that although there were similarities and a certain amount of cross-Atlantic influences at work, there were also differences. The craft of making quilts, which obviously went out to North America with the emigrants from the British Isles, flourished in the New World, but in a different soil. The repeating block, for example, never really caught on in Britain, with the exception of the Log Cabin pattern; in the United States, the block pattern became a standard basis of design. Embroidery also played a more profound role in British quiltmaking, especially in the use of decorative (as opposed to utilitarian) quilting.

Chambers Twentieth Century Dictionary defines a quilt as 'a bed-cover of two thicknesses with padding sewn in compartments'. For the purposes of this book I have adopted a broader interpretation and included coverlets which display techniques that are of interest to contemporary quiltmakers. In any event, one of the quirks of British quilting, patchwork and appliqué is that often only two layers of fabric were used: there was no filling (in the example of Broderie Perse, only one layer).

There are a number of fine quilts in British museums. Unfortunately, a general lack of space and resources keeps most of Britain's quilt treasures from the public view. In order to appreciate the extent of any museum collection it is necessary to make an appointment to view. Even then the serious student is more likely to see photographic slides of the collection than the actual quilts. This is not only due (and rightly so) to conservation measures on the part of curatorial staff, but also to the fact that unpacking textiles from storage requires considerable time. This celebration of British quilts attempts to overcome these difficulties, at the same time recording the rich diversity of the craft as it was practised by women and men in Ireland, Scotland, England and Wales.

For permitting me to try their patience and pick their brains, I am deeply indebted to Linda Ballard, Textile Curator of the Ulster Folk and Transport Museum, Holywood; Clare Rose, Keeper of Costume and Textiles, York Castle Museum; and Liz Arthur, Assistant Keeper of Costume, City of Glasgow Museums and Art Galleries. My thanks also go to Rosemary E. Allan, Keeper of Social History, Beamish North of England Open Air Museum, Stanley; Janice Murray, Keeper of Human History, City of Dundee Museums and Art Galleries; R. Ross Noble, Curator of the Highland Folk Museum, Kingussie; Fiona Strodder, Assistant Keeper of Social History, Norfolk Museums Service; A. Lloyd Hughes, Archivist, Welsh Folk Museum, St Fagans; the Scottish Women's Rural Institutes; Elizabeth McCrum, Assistant Keeper, Ulster Museum, Belfast; to collectors Ron Simpson, London; Ann Carswell, Edinburgh; and Jen Jones, Llanybydder, Dyfed, Wales; and to my husband Bill Rae.

For the opportunity to transform the idea of an illustrated book about British quilts into reality, I am deeply grateful to Ib Bellew. And for proving that no photographic assignment is impossible – even a quilt from the top of scaffolding – my special thanks go to David Cripps.

Janet Rae
Edinburgh, 1987

Turkey Red and white pineapple Log Cabin quilt made in
Ireland about 1875. 6 ft 7 in × 6 ft 8 in (201 cm × 203 cm).
(Ulster Folk and Transport Museum)

Introduction

The quest for antique needlework of any description is filled with joy and frustration. For the quilt addict, the joy comes with the discovery of a long-sought curiosity, like a Bible quilt, or the opportunity to examine a particularly fine example of piecing. The frustration develops with the thumbing of old exhibition catalogues and the realization that the passage of time (plus moths and neglect) has claimed some items for ever.

Exhibitions are a good excuse to exhume old family treasures from the attic, and to show off one's own needle skills. In the case of quilts, exhibitions of bygone years furnish evidence of certain fashions in the craft. The Great Exhibition of 1851 at Crystal Palace, for example, had a number of contemporary patchwork and quilting entries. E.A. Penley of Margate submitted a box patchwork table cover which contained over 2,000 pieces of silk and 500,000 stitches. Fourteen-year-old Clara Pearse of Bath showed a crocheted bed-quilt illustrated with the Ten Commandments, and Elizabeth Barnes of Oxford, who was an invalid, exhibited a quilt which contained 9,851 hexagons in wool (each the size of a shilling) and a quilted border of amber-coloured satin. There were others that also arouse one's curiosity: a seven-foot square table cover which contained 30,000 pieces of broadcloth; several embroidered quilts, not well described; and a quilt knitted by the inmates of Richmond Lunatic Asylum.

Antique quilts are also of interest if they are well documented and have historical associations. When the Edinburgh Museum of Science and Art (now the Royal Museum of Scotland, Chambers Street) held an exhibition of art needlework in 1877, it included a number of quilted bed-covers, new and old, as well as a silk quilt with a central pastoral embroidery and a border of flowers. The quilt was alleged to have once covered the bed of Archbishop Sharp, presumably Archbishop Sharp of St Andrews, well-known persecutor of the Presbyterian Covenanters, who met an untimely end in 1679; a party of fugitive Covenanters dragged him from his coach on the lonely Magus Muir between Cupar and St Andrews and put him to death.

On a lighter note, the National Exhibition of Needlework by the Scottish Women's Rural Institutes at the Royal Scottish Academy, Edinburgh, in 1934, contained a quilted skirt in red satin which had been worn by Margaret Murray, wife of Robert Graham, 11th Laird of Fintry, at the Court of Prince Charles Edward Stuart at Holyrood Palace in 1745, and also by her great-grand-daughter, Anne Carnegy, Mrs Soutar, at an Assembly held by Queen Victoria in Edinburgh. And in the same exhibition was a quilt about which the maker modestly expressed misgivings in a historic letter:

. . . Ye counterpaine I hope you will lick. I had itt work'd a purpose, & I desire you will except itt from me as a small mark of my shewing you of my respect for your oblidging manner of living with me here. I don't know how to tell you, madame, what a sense I have of your shewing a concern in our affairs, which all has not done ye same.

Don't think this quilt fine for tis a poore business and you will be disappointed when you see it, but since I writ, I could not help tell you my thoughts in some manner . . .

This letter, written on 19 October 1700 by the Countess of Orkney, was addressed to her sister-in-law, the Countess of Tullibardine. Regrettably, the 'poore business' – the quilt – was not described further.

Quiltmaking in Britain has enough of these anecdotes to invest the craft with an interesting and varied history. Needlework of every description – domestic as well as costume – does, of course, figure prominently in the country's heritage. Facility with the needle was at one time considered akin to virtue. A letter written to *The Spectator* magazine in the eighteenth century describes one woman's concern about what she perceived as a decline of interest in needlework:

I have a couple of nieces under my direction who so often run gadding abroad that I do not know where to have them. Their dress, their tea, and their visits take up all their time and they go to bed as tired doing nothing, as I am often after quilting a whole under-petticoat.[1]

The letter-writer's plea to *The Spectator* to recommend the 'long-neglected art of needlework' obviously fell on sympathetic ears, for the editor replied that needlework was one way of keeping women away from the scandalous gossip of the tea table. He also argued that the 'pretty arts' had to be encouraged, and made the following proposals to 'all mothers in Great Britain':

1. That no young virgin whatsoever be allowed to receive the addresses of her first lover, but in a suit of her own embroidering.
2. That before every fresh humble servant she shall be obliged to appear with a new stomacher at the least.
3. That no one be actually married until she hath the child-bed pillows, etc, ready stitched, as likewise the mantle for the boy quite finished.
These laws, if I mistake not, would effectually restore the decaying art of needlework, and make the virgins of Great Britain exceedingly nimble-fingered in their business.[2]

What the virgins of Britain thought about these eighteenth-century words of advice is, regrettably, unrecorded. Sewing, in any event, was not intended as a device to keep young women from mischief: it was a necessity even in middle-class households, and from the evidence available we have to assume, with Elizabeth Glaister, that 'no piece of secular needlework gave our ancestresses more satisfaction, both in the making and when made, as the quilt or bed-coverlet'.[3]

The making of quilts captured the attention of many women, whether they were poor and trying to keep warm by recycling old clothes and blankets into utility covers, or whether they were living in middle-class comfort and in need of some type of needle activity to fill their time. Certainly there were some very intriguing individuals who elected to make quilts: in addition to a long line of noble ladies who included quilting among their many needlework accomplishments, there was the indefatigable Elizabeth Fry, who took patchwork piecing and embroidery into Newgate Prison in 1816, and whose story is told in Chapter 5. And there was also the gregarious Mrs Delany, whose six volumes of autobiography and letters provide insights into her life in Ireland and the English Court of George III in the eighteenth century. One of Mrs Delany's quilts, made in 1750, was of linen and decorated with life-sized flowers that had been worked in coloured silks in a running stitch. A coverlet by Mrs Delany, the only complete piece of her embroidery known to have survived, is in the collection of the Ulster Museum in Belfast. It is also of Irish linen and has been worked with knotted and couched cream cord in a design which features a central medallion of flowers surrounded by a trellis of flowerheads.

Men also had a role in piecing and designing quilts in Britain. In the seventeenth and eighteenth centuries the role of the limner was very important to ladies of the noble households, for he it was who composed their designs and drew them out on cloth. In the nineteenth century, George Gardiner, a shopkeeper in Northumberland, performed the same function for the local women who wanted a quilt top marked for working. The idea that an artist was essential to embroidery or quilt design was also embraced in the Art Needlework movement of the nineteenth century: women were advised to use the services of an artist if they could not themselves draw, or even to go to the Royal School of Art Needlework in London, where they could borrow designs that had already been worked. One supporter of the Art Needlework movement, Lewis Day, even went so far as to suggest that women were incapable of designing: they should do the stitchery, he said, and leave the designing to the men! It has to be acknowledged, however, that some men proved equally adept with the needle. Pieced table covers and inlay work, of the type described in Chapter 4, were a highlight of the Great Exhibition of 1851 and many of these entries were by men. Soldiers, sailors and tailors also seemed particularly attracted by the challenge of intricate piecing.

British quilts made prior to 1935 are generally considered to fall into one of three categories: the frame quilt, which usually consisted of a medallion centre, either pieced or appliquéd, surrounded by borders; the mosaic quilt, a slight misnomer which was universally used to describe geometric piecing or inlay work; and the quilted cover, which relies on the quilting for its artistry rather than on the piecing or appliqué. None of these categories, however, allows for the quilted covers decorated with crewel work or fine embroidery or corded work, which was sometimes executed in blue thread on white – all techniques popular in the eighteenth century. The block system of assembly and design, which developed in North America, was never widely used in Britain except for the Log Cabin pattern. (In Ireland, interestingly, when blocks were used as a unit of design in the middle of the nineteenth century, they were called 'panes'. A reminiscence about a pieced blue and white quilt of triangles, set together in a Double T panel of five-inch squares, is in the files of the Ulster Folk and Transport Museum. The same source, who recalled work done in a previous generation, also described a tulip appliqué quilt in red and green on ten-inch panes.)

Quilts were made in all parts of the British Isles but the craft flourished particularly in Ireland, Wales and the north of England. Wales, Durham and Northumberland developed a reputation for fine quilting and making whole cloth and strip quilts (the latter are called stripy quilts locally). The Irish preferred appliqué and piecing: quilting was not enthusiastically embraced by them, except as a necessity, and when used it was normally executed in the wave pattern. The Scots did make quilts, but not in quantity, their reputation for applied work lying more in the direction of embroidery. Nor can the influence of embroidery be ignored in any investigation of British quiltmaking. Historically the techniques of quilting, appliqué and piecing were considered part of the embroiderer's remit. Quilting as both a decorative and functional stitch was practised with great skill in the eighteenth and early nineteenth centuries, as was appliqué, although the latter was usually employed in making coverlets of a single thickness. Piecing as a technique actually fell into a certain disrepute in some quarters during the early nineteenth century, but was revived by the Victorians.

Dorinda, praising the virtues of patchwork in 1883, commented that although it had once been practised only as a means of using up scraps or teaching children to sew, it 'has lately become quite a favourite work and though it is becoming more elaborate and more difficult, it is at the same time far more satisfactory and if well arranged is particularly effective'.[4] By 1928, one stitchery expert was downright contemptuous: 'Patchwork can hardly attain to a high position amongst the various branches of embroidery,' sniffed Mrs Archibald Christie in The Artistic Crafts Series of Technical Handbooks, edited by W.R. Lethaby. Lethaby in a previous publication had commented that patchwork had been spoiled for a time by 'being narrowed down to the box pattern'.[5]

The way in which quilts were used in Britain and the social status of the maker also has considerable bearing on quilt design historically. The spartan interior of a Durham or Welsh miner's cottage would be considerably enhanced by a red quilted whole cloth cover; it would provide both the warmth of a blanket and a certain decorative quality. Appliquéd coverlets, on the other hand, were more for 'show'. Among the middle classes, too – those who could afford to own more than one quilt – the element of fashion was also present as was sometimes a distinction between 'summer' and 'winter' bedding.

The word 'quilt', in the late nineteenth century, was used to describe almost any type of top covering used on a bed. In the instance of a 'summer' quilt, this could mean, in reality, a large linen sheet, without backing, which had been decorated with embroidery or appliqué, sometimes edged with fringe. It could also mean a single layer of Turkey Red, decorated with white cross stitch. One type of stitchery that became popular for summer quilts during their period of popularity was 'damask work', which was executed on small squares and then joined with bands of lace or Turkey Red twill. Damask work was embroidery on top of damask, with the stitches usually forming an outline around the woven design. A more elaborate version of the work, however, was also undertaken on pale silk brocade, in which case the embroidery design was superimposed.

Winter quilts, which provided greater warmth, could be made of serge or thin cloth and filled for additional warmth. The 'blanket quilt' was also a useful possibility during the late nineteenth century: it was nothing more than a blanket around which scalloped edges were worked in buttonhole stitch. Sometimes there was a central design in crewel embroidery and a border of cotton velvet in a contrasting colour. Or perhaps strips of cretonne would be applied for decoration. To ensure that such a quilt really provided warmth, sheets of brown paper were tacked to the edges and red flannel attached as a lining. For children, an inexpensive quilt could also be made by quilting together three or four old, thin blankets or by making a quick cover of puff patchwork – joining up small squares of scraps which had been sewn separately and stuffed with frayed or fragmented woollen scraps or even bits of torn paper.

Another curiosity of the 1870s was the practice of partially covering either an eiderdown quilt or quilted woollen counterpane. Such covers or linings were placed on the underside of the quilt and fashioned with scalloped edges which buttoned around the top edges. The famous Mrs Beeton, known primarily as a cook, wrote only one book on needlework, and in it she recommended just such a cover: in particular she suggested a quilted counterpane of scarlet cashmere, with a white linen lining, which had been suitably embroidered in buttonhole, satin, and ladder stitch. The lining, with scalloped edges, was to be attached to the quilt with mother-of-pearl buttons.[6] *Sylvia's Home Journal* in 1879 suggested a similar project: an eiderdown quilt with a cover of blue silk embroidered with satin and buttonhole stitches, threaded with grosgrain ribbon and decorated with lace.

These eccentricities of British quiltmaking may strike the contemporary quilter as mere quirks. A quilt, after all, is supposed to contain two layers of cloth with a filling between and be stitched in such a way that all three layers are held together. Bed-covers, however, were as much prey to fashion as was costume. Many a housewife would have discarded a patchwork quilt to make way for the new machine-made Marcella covers in the late nineteenth century. Likewise, in this century, fine quilted whole cloth quilts would have been stored away to make room for the more up-to-date chenille. Fortunately, enough antique quilts have survived to give us a good idea of how the craft was practised in Britain. They tell us that men and women living a hundred or two hundred years ago derived as much pleasure from quiltmaking as do the needleworkers of today.

Notes

1. Countess of Wilton, *The Art of Needlework,* London, 1840, p.351.
2. Ibid., p.353.
3. E. Glaister, *Needlework,* London, 1880, p.96.
4. Dorinda, *Needlework for Ladies for Pleasure and Profit,* London, 1883, p.24.
5. W.R. Lethaby, *Home and Country Arts,* London, 1923.
6. *Beeton's Book of Needlework*, London: Ward Lock, 1870.

1

QUILTERS AND QUILTING

The history of quilting in Britain shows two diverse uses for the technique: utilitarian and ornamental. The notion that two layers of cloth, filled and stitched, could be used for both warmth and protection stretches far back into history. In Britain it gained credence during medieval times when undergarments were needed to protect men from the discomfort of armour. Indeed, the practical usefulness of quilting in relation to costume has been recognized from that day to this.

In the British Isles quilting and its evolution are also related to social class. All of the early records in which quilts are mentioned relate to royal or noble households, where embroidery was both practised and cherished, and where quilting was regarded as another branch of the embroiderer's skill. Use of the quilting technique in this instance contrasts sharply with the quilting used on utilitarian bed-covers. Women in poorer households also quilted but more for economy than in pursuit of artistry – though that too developed, in its own distinct way, in Wales and the north of England.

In so far as quilting was used as a technique to make bedding, there are references in British records as far back as the fourteenth century and the *Romance of Arthur of Lytel Brytayne,* where mention is made of a 'rich quylt wrought with coten, with crimson sendel silken stuff stitched with thredes of golde'.[1] Other records show that quilts were fairly common in the homes of royalty and nobility from the sixteenth century onwards: Henry VIII, for example, not only had quilts of gold and silver, he once gave twenty-three quilts to Katharine Howard as a sign of his favour.

In Elizabethan England (1558–1603), where the embroiderer's art flourished not only in costume but in the domestic sector as well, one of the most important and luxurious features of a noble household was the bed. The embroiderer's art was applied not only to the hangings of the four-posters, but to the valances, the pillows and the coverlets. Rich fabrics were used, including silk and velvet, and white linen too became an ideal ground on which to execute different types of stitchery. Quilting was very much part of the embroiderer's art during this era, used as a background, and often 'gamboised' – executed in diamond-shaped checks. Corded or Italian quilting was also very popular in the seventeenth century and was often employed in combination with stuffed quilting. Its popularity, however, went into something of a decline in the eighteenth century.

In the late 1600s a preference also grew for using yellow silk or gold thread in background quilting, possibly, it is said, in imitation of the coverlets that were coming into the country from the Dutch East Indies. Eastern quilting was also imitated in the adaptation of vermicular (i.e. serpentine) quilting (also in yellow or gold) as a background stitch. Embroidered coverlets with a vermicular pattern had been imported from the Portuguese colony of Goa in the seventeenth century.

The use of yellow or gold thread in decorative background quilting continued to be popular for some time, and fortunately a number of these quilts are still in existence, including several in the Victoria and Albert Museum in London dating from the late seventeenth century. Quilting is said to have reached its pinnacle during the reign of Queen Anne (1702–14) and her name is still associated with one type of quilting stitch, the back stitch, which was generally used through the top layer and wadding but not the backing. Queen Anne quilting was sometimes called 'pseudo' quilting because it did not penetrate all three layers of cloth. That type of quilting, which could very well be interpreted as

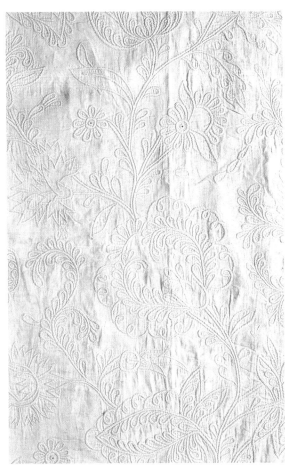

Right: Detail of white linen corded coverlet made about 1790. 6 ft 6 in × 7 ft 1 in (198 cm × 216 cm). (Ulster Folk and Transport Museum)

Far right: Early eighteenth-century white linen corded coverlet. 7 ft 11 in × 8 ft 1 in (241 cm × 246 cm). (Strangers' Hall, Norfolk Museums Service)

Below: Section of late seventeenth-century coverlet with vermicular background in Queen Anne quilting. Embroidered on natural ground with yellow floss silk with feathers and fronds worked in chain stitch, satin stitch and buttonhole. 3 ft 9 in × 5 ft 6 in (114 cm × 168 cm). (Strangers' Hall Norfolk Museums Service).

embroidery, especially if a coloured thread was used, was employed on some types of fine quilting (especially silk and domette), and in fact was still being taught in the Wemyss School of Needlework in Scotland in the 1940s.

The quilt made by Martha Lennox of Belfast in 1712 is a superb illustration of how decorative background quilting was used with fine embroidery, though in this case the thread used for the quilting was pale green silk from France (see page 15). The back stitch quilting is executed through two layers of fabric and each quilted diamond is roughly one half-inch across. The Lennox quilt has survived in excellent condition, chiefly because it was categorized as 'household linen' and passed down through the female line of the family. Martha McTier, who inherited it in 1800, described the circumstances in which her aunt, Miss Martha Young, gave her the quilt:

I was sent for to her [Miss Young] the same morning, but found it was to show me a very valuable and curious quilt wrought by her grandmother and which was the wonder of its day near a hundred years ago – the coloured silks it is wrought in cost 30£. This same quilt she told me Hamilton desired might be given to me – she therefore

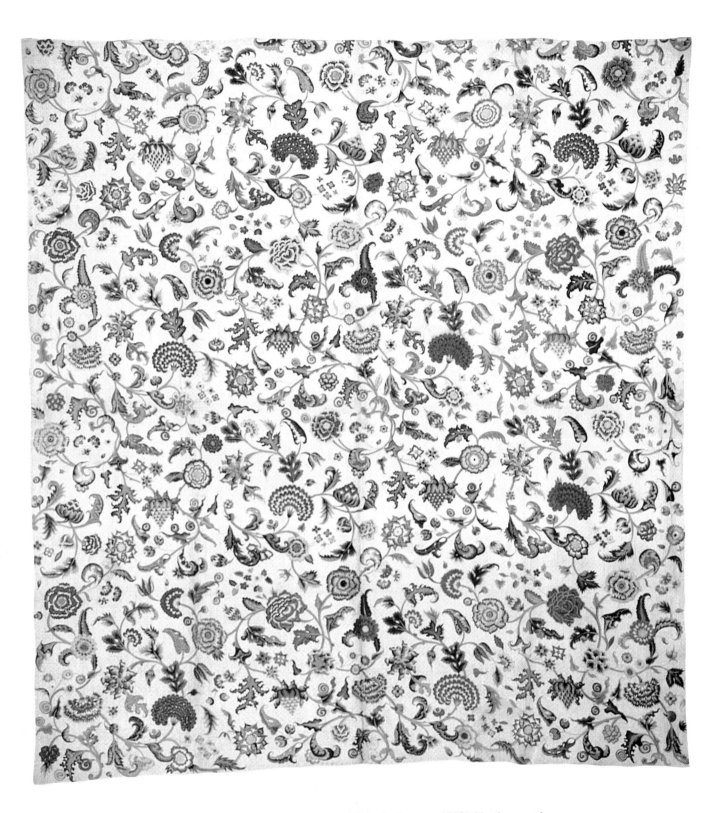

The Lennox quilt. Signed and dated 'Martha Lennox 1712'. Martha was the daughter of John Hamilton, the first Sovereign (Mayor) of Belfast, who died in 1686. Martha died in 1729 at about the age of forty-three. The embroidered flowers, which show a great skill in colour blending and matching, are executed in long and short stitch, stem stitch, French knots and laidwork. The abrupt ending of the pattern on one side suggests the quilt was cut down at some stage.
6 ft × 6 ft 6 in (183 cm × 198 cm). (Ulster Museum)

Above: Section of the Lennox quilt showing both embroidered flowers and the quilted background. The quilt has no filling but a very fine backing.

Below: Corner of early eighteenth-century stuffed and corded quilt in canary yellow silk taffeta with linen backing. 6 ft square (183 cm). (Strangers' Hall, Norfolk Museums Service)

did so, to do with as I chose so it did not go out of the family. Sarah will take it along with the House linen which I have not yet seen, but by its weight and bulk I suppose is valuable.[2]

Another embroidered quilt on record was treated less kindly, as this entry from a 1934 exhibition catalogue testifies:

Quilt worked in silk and gold on linen. Quilted background. This quilt matches the firescreen worked in 1699 by Lady Margaret Hamilton, wife of James, fourth Lord Panmure, and daughter of William, third Duke of Hamilton and Anne, Duchess of Hamilton. When found at Colstoun in 1860 by Lady Susan Ramsay, it was being used as a table cloth in the visiting footman's room, who had spilt a bottle of ink over it, thus causing the black stain.[3]

Many of the quilts that have survived from the eighteenth century are of linen, quilted with silk or linen thread. Some are decorated with embroidery or crewel work, with the quilting done in a white running stitch ('runnings'). The Treasurer's House in York, a property owned by the National Trust, has an excellent example of a linen bed-cover with crewel embroidery and background quilting. It is commonly believed that the embroidery on these types of quilts was undertaken after the background quilting had been completed. This was not always the case: the quilt on page 17, which was made from a cut-down quilt and the addition of a border, was quilted from the back. The quilting stitches go through the crewel flowers.

Machine-made cotton Marcella, which was quilted in a diamond pattern and sold by the yard, appeared in the latter half of the nineteenth century. It is said to have had a deleterious effect on the hand-made variety of quilt. Yet the use of embroidery for bed-covers resurfaced as a popular fashion, when art needlework became the vogue (see Chapter 4 on appliqué). That movement, of course, reintroduced many of the designs of earlier centuries and, by this time, a rudimentary form of time-and-motion study seemed to be entering the creation of new work. Embroidery was promoted as the main creative technique and the idea of a quilted background, while admired, was not deemed worthy of inclusion. M.S. Lockwood, on defining the meaning of the word quilt, commented:

In these days, and with a decorative end in view, such very elaborate work hardly repays the time spent on it; but we do recommend the coverlet as an excellent object for work and design. Outline work in one colour is very suitable for this purpose, and a bold formal pattern looks very handsome. A more flowing and branching design, well enclosed in lines and borders will look equally well.[4]

Bolton sheeting was recommended as the foundation for such a coverlet, and both appliqué and crewel work advocated as the techniques to be used on designs which resembled elaborate curved wrought-iron work with infills of flowers and leaves.

E. Glaister was equally contemptuous of quilting two years later. After commenting on the work of previous centuries she said:

Perhaps the best result as a work of art was attained when both quilting and flowers were done in bright yellow silk, the effect of this colour on a white ground being always particularly good.

There is so much to be done in this century besides needlework, even by the most industrious workers, that such labours as these cannot be advised, except perhaps on a small scale for a cot or cradle.[5]

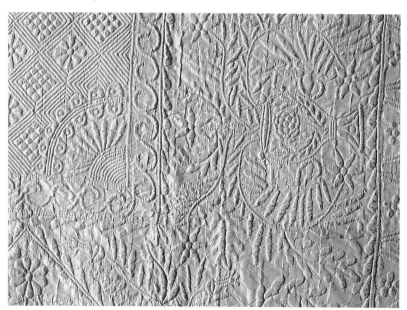

She suggested a rather elaborate design based on an old English quilt as a project. Four-inch circles of trailing tulips with daisy infills were to be embroidered on fine linen in several different embroidery stitches – a project which if simplified and finished with a quilted ground would have been made in far less time.

At the beginning of the present century, Mrs Archibald Christie expressed support for the previous attitude that quilting was only suitable as background: 'It is wonderful to see the improvement made in a floral design by working a geometrical pattern in outline over the ground.'[6]

Mrs Christie offered as an example an old quilt dated 1703 which had a vase of flowers embroidered in the centre and a quilting pattern in white back stitch. More remarkable was her description of the quilting pattern that had been executed in the border – it included fish in water, a church, a three-masted ship, a horse and crested moon, a griffin, a dragon among foliage, a castle, a dog and rabbit, a mermaid holding a comb and mirror, a lion and peacock and a shield of arms with initials.

The revival of quilting in Durham and Wales in the 1920s, explained later in this chapter, also had a knock-on effect beyond this particular craft industry. Coats Clark of Glasgow, the manufacturers of thread, proclaimed the virtues of quilting in the May 1927 issue of their magazine, *The Needlewoman*. An article entitled 'Quilting and its Newest Developments' opens thus:

Once more a cycle of fashion has been completed, and quilting, which had a vogue in our great-grandmother's day for the making of cosy coverlets and petticoats, again invades the realms of dress, but this time makes its appeal through decorative qualities rather than for its power of giving warmth.

The magazine article advocated not only corded quilting, but quilting as a suitable embellishment for the hems of taffeta 'frocks' and cloth coats. The running stitch, back stitch and chain stitch using silk or stranded cotton was suggested, as was the desirability of quilting a border which had a diaper (diamond) pattern as the background.

Five years after this promotion of decorative quilting in costume, the authors of *Modern Needlecraft* commented in 1933: 'Quilting is a method of embroidery whereby three layers of material are held together.'[7] They resurrected a very old curiosity in quiltmaking: 'eyelet holes too are a valuable addition as they assist ventilation and form an extra unit of design.' A white cot quilt made with this technique and dating from the pre-World

War II era is in the collection of the Scottish Women's Rural Institutes. It is a fine example of quilting used as both a functional and a decorative stitch. The quilting has been done in blue thread and the eyelet or pierced holes embroidered with blue buttonhole stitch.

Left: The centre of an early eighteenth-century linen quilt embellished with crewel embroidery. 7 ft × 7 ft 7 in (213 cm × 231 cm). (Glasgow School of Art)

Below: Section of cot quilt, made about 1935, which features pierced quilting using buttonhole stitch. 2 ft × 3 ft (61 cm × 91 cm). (Scottish Women's Rural Institutes)

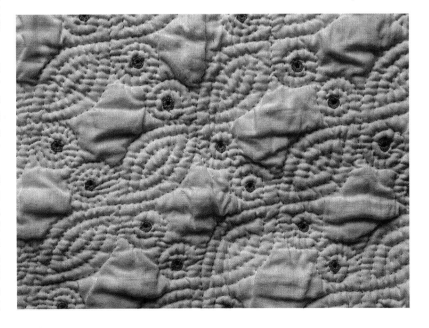

PROFESSIONAL QUILTERS

Quilting as a paid occupation probably grew in step with the professions of embroidering and tailoring, but it is also known to have been associated with upholstery: quilted fabric was used as a lining for coach interiors in the eighteenth century as well as for beds. Some of the quilting specialists in the eighteenth century concentrated solely on petticoats which, like dressmaking, proved singularly unrewarding. A reference to the quilters' profession in *The London Tradesman* of 1747 commented on their meagre earnings:

They [quilters] quilt likewise Quilts for Beds for the upholder. This they make more of than the Petticoats, but nothing very considerable, nothing to get rich by, unless they are able to purchase the materials and sell them finished to the Shops, which few of them do. They rarely take apprentices, and the Women they employ to help them, earn Three to Four Shillings a Week and their Diet.[8]

By the nineteenth century, professional quilters had a more definite role, especially in the north of England and Wales where the art of quilting, as we know it today, flourished. Mavis Fitzrandolph (whose book *Traditional Quilting*[9] gives a valuable insight into the social status of these quilting practitioners), divided the professionals into three categories: the village quilters, the itinerant quilters and the quilters who ran quilt clubs in the mining communities. To these should be added a fourth category – the professional quilt markers or stampers, who were paid solely for their designs and not for their needle skills, although they sometimes exercised these also.

Walter Gale, a Sussex schoolmaster who lived in the mid-eighteenth century, was an example of a quilt marker. He supplemented his income from teaching by marking quilt patterns, some of which may have been for corded quilts, drawing embroidery patterns for waistcoats, and by painting signs. It would sometimes take as long as a week for him to complete the marking of one quilt top, and for this he was paid less than a pound.

In the latter part of the nineteenth century George Gardiner, a shopkeeper in the village of Allenheads in Northumberland, also gained a reputation as a quilt stamper. He passed his skill on to his two nieces (also teaching them to quilt), as well as a number of other pupils, the best known being Elizabeth Sanderson who died in 1934. Elizabeth's reputation eventually outshone that of her mentor. She marked quilt tops with a blue pencil and was able to complete two in a day for which she was paid from one shilling and sixpence to two shillings and sixpence ($7\frac{1}{2}$p to $12\frac{1}{2}$p) each, the sum presumably depending on the size and complexity of design.

Many of the tops marked by the stampers still retain the marks of the blue pencil. Elizabeth was also a quilter: the star quilt, one of her typical patterns, is shown on page 19. The marking of quilts continued to be a professional skill practised by a few North Country stampers right through the 1970s, although by that time there was little call for it.

Quilting in the 1800s was a skill often practised as a sideline to dressmaking, and village quilters also took apprentices – at least in Wales. Mrs Fitzrandolph recorded one instance where parents paid a £2 fee for their daughter to be trained. The girl lived with the quilter during her year's training, so presumably the money helped towards her board. One of the most amazing village quilters on record was Mary Jones of Wales who died about 1900. She was ambidextrous and, working with an apprentice, could make as many as two quilts in a week, compared to the usual output of one in a fortnight. Customers brought Mary their own material for quilting and she was usually paid between four and six shillings (20p and 30p) for her work.

Itinerant quilters, who sometimes carried their own frames, were paid between sixpence and one shilling ($2\frac{1}{2}$p and 5p) a day around the beginning of the twentieth century. They travelled from farm to farm in the north of England and in Wales, and often their quilting skills were offered along with dressmaking. One Welsh itinerant quilter actually specialized in making dowry quilts. Travelling quilters were also known in the Scottish Borders and in Ireland, where sometimes they offered their services as knitters as well. County Fermanagh had a 'Johnny Quilt' in the nineteenth century and in the same country a whole family were known as the Quilts because of their pursuit of this craft.[10]

Of all the professional quilters in northern England, however, the one who earned the most notable spot in quilting history was Joe Hedley, 'Joe the Quilter' (also called the Hermit of Warden). He lived and worked in a small thatched cottage in the village of Warden in Northumberland in the nineteenth century. Joe had trained as a tailor, but his real reputation for stitchery was acquired as a quilter. He designed and quilted (one of his quilts is pictured on page 20) on both linen and cotton, and kept handy a stock of cardboard patterns from

Eight-point medallion star within a star, stamped by
Elizabeth Sanderson of Allenheads, Northumberland, about
1900. A star surrounded by borders was typical of the work
done by this well-known North Country marker, and in this
example she used chains, flowers and shells for the quilting
patterns. 7 ft 1 in × 7 ft 4 in (216 cm × 224 cm). (Beamish
North of England Open Air Museum)

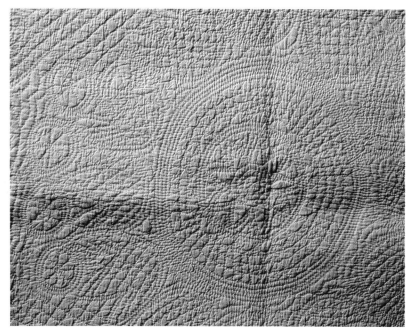

Central detail of white cotton quilt made by Joe Hedley about 1820. Quilted at one-half inch intervals with a running stitch. The quilt has been reduced from its original size but still measures 8 ft 2 in × 5 ft 4 in (249 cm × 163 cm). (Beamish North of England Open Air Museum)

which his customers could select. His quilting was very fine – sometimes executed at quarter-inch intervals – and he was partial to flowers, chains and diamond shapes, which he outlined on quilt tops with either chalk or pencil.

Joe's character is well described in *The Monthly Chronicle of North-Country Lore and Legend,* published in 1887, a book which described Joe's untimely end as a 'terrible and mysterious tragedy'. According to the legend, Joe led a blameless and Christian life, nursed his ailing wife for eight years until she died, and grew gooseberries in a garden he had reclaimed from a piece of wasteland. Joe's cottage was isolated and, aside from the young lovers who frequented his gooseberry patch, his other social contacts were primarily wandering pedlars and beggars who stopped to pass the time of day and relate the latest stories of the road. It was the cottage's isolation that led to Joe's terrible end . . . that and the belief by persons unknown that he had accumulated a tidy sum of money from his quilting.

Joe was discovered by his neighbours one day in 1826 in a pool of blood, with forty-four wounds to his body, some inflicted with a knife and some with a rake. The details of his murder were horrific. Though aged seventy-six, he had put up a stout struggle with his attackers, for his bloody fingerprints were found throughout his cottage and even in the lane outside, to which it was believed he had escaped before being dragged back indoors. What little furniture he had was broken, and to complete the grisly tale, blood and hairs were found on the doorway lintel where his head had struck.

A number of people were arrested after the crime but no one was convicted. The parish, which had been giving Joe financial help, offered a reward of one hundred guineas to whoever would bring the guilty person to justice. The Home Secretary, Sir Robert Peel, offered a free pardon to any but the actual murderer who would give information leading to a conviction. It was all to no avail – Joe's murderers were never found, although in later years one or two people are said to have confessed to the crime. His cottage was pulled down in 1872.

Such was the notoriety of the dastardly deed that Joe soon became part of local legend, and a poet named Wright was moved to compose a poem of no less than twenty-four verses chronicling Joe's end. A few stanzas convey the flavour of the work:

His quilts with country fame were crown'd,
So neatly stitch'd, and all the ground
Adorn'd with flowers, or figured round,
Oh, clever Joe the Quilter!

His friends, his hens, his cat and garden,
He never thought his lot a hard one;
And the old Hermit of High Warden,
They called good Joe the Quilter.

Oft in his solitary nook,
With shaking head, but steadfast look.
Through spectacles on goodly book,
Was seen the pious Quilter.

His lowly latch was thought secure,
At night he seldom ope'd the door,
Except to lodge the wand'ring poor–
Oh! hospitable Quilter.

Who raised the tale 'twere vain to scan,
But far and wide the story ran
That there was scarce a wealthier man
Than poor old Joe the Quilter.

Satan by this vain tale, 'tis said,
Had put it in some monster's head
To violate the lowly shed,
And murder Joe the Quilter.

Missed by his friends at Walwick Grange,
Who thought his few days' absence strange,
They sought the cot—and—awful change,
There lay the murdered Quilter.

We pass the horrid scene of blood,
For when hath feeling hearts withstood
The grief of the afflicted good?
All mourned for Joe the Quilter.

Know, then, ye proud ones of the earth,
How light weigh greatness, wealth, and birth,
To lowly virtue's heavenly worth,
And envy Joe the Quilter.[11]

Pieced sawtooth stars of red, beige and blue floral printed cotton on white, with a sawtooth border. The quilting pattern of rose and cross has been sewn from the reverse side. Made about 1890. 6 ft 7 in square (210 cm). (Beamish North of England Open Air Museum)

QUILT CLUBS

Life in the mining communities of Wales and northern England was very hard in the nineteenth century, even in comparison to the rest of Britain. Collieries by the dozen were founded, each modest pit supported by its own village. In most instances, the local colliery was the only significant source of employment. Virtually every villager was dependent on the coal owner for his livelihood, and if anything happened to the family's chief wage earner, then the widow either had to depend on her neighbours or what little she could earn from doing laundry, dressmaking or quilting. Pensions and welfare benefits still lay a long way in the future.

Quilting seemed to flourish in this difficult environment. Communities were extremely close-knit and loyal to their own, but the domestic living conditions were such that one wonders where space was found to put the quilting frames. The houses in these small mining communities were built either of brick or stone and most were constructed in a terraced row, each cottage with an outside toilet (or 'netty'). The houses usually had small vegetable gardens and often a pigeon loft, for the breeding and racing of homing pigeons was a favourite hobby of miners. Though small, the houses were invariably warm and snug, since miners had a concessionary coal supply in addition to their wages. The kitchen range, kept highly polished with blacklead, was a focal point. Furnishings were sparse, chiefly because of a lack of space. Families were usually large, and often a number of children would be accommodated in one bed – the 'dess' bed which folded into a wall recess during the day.

Given the domestic restrictions and the hardships of living, the elaborate and decorative quilting practised by the miners' wives is all the more remarkable. There are many records of women who raised large families following the death of a husband in the pits – women who achieved the impossible because of the money, however little, they could earn quilting. This dependence on quilting continued into the twentieth century. Mrs Ellen Robson of County Durham, for example, was a miner's widow who raised nine children. She could complete a quilt in two weeks and the quilts sold for ten shillings (50p) each. Another was Mrs Sally Ranson, of New Seaham, County Durham, whose quilt is pictured on page 23. She too was a miner's widow who raised a family of four: she was born in 1870 and lived to the age of eighty-six.

The economic constrictions on the miners' families were undoubtedly responsible for the origin of the quilt clubs, which are believed to have started in Wales, in County Durham and Northumberland in the latter part of the nineteenth century. The clubs were a practical solution to the problem of buying cotton and wadding since they were operated on the instalment plan. Regular payments of one shilling (5p) a week for twenty weeks made to the quilter, over a period, not only provided her with an income and the money for materials, it gave the purchaser of the quilt time to pay. Each club member received a completed quilt in rotation. One of the most unusual quilts made in one of these clubs in the early twentieth century was quilted by Mrs Stewart of Bowburn, County Durham. It is reversible, one side having a plain cream centre with a blue and cream print border, and the other a plain pink centre with a pink and cream print border. The quilted centrepiece includes flowers, leaves and the wineglass pattern while the outer border has a running feather. The quilt is in the collection of the North of England Open Air Museum, Beamish.

The north of England, during the nineteenth century, was also a citadel of Methodism. John Wesley, its founder, had travelled widely on horseback in the region during the previous century, preaching, converting and organizing. For untold numbers of ordinary people, the Methodist chapel became a vital part of their lives, the services providing both solace and evangelistic fervour. Clubs which produced both quilts and rag rugs also became associated with these chapels, the monies earned being used for chapel funds. Indeed, it was often said that many a chapel was built on quilts.

RURAL INDUSTRIES BUREAU

Quilting as a craft in Wales and Durham experienced a revival in 1921, a time of industrial strikes and great economic deprivation, following the establishment of the Rural Industries Bureau.

The Bureau was financed by the Development Fund but itself had no funds to allocate: rather its function was to give advice on development and to disseminate information about small factories

White cotton quilt with printed border made by Mrs Sally
Ranson of New Seaham, County Durham, about 1890. Mrs
Ranson, a miner's widow, raised a family of four children by
quilting and by running a quilting club. She died in 1956 at
the age of eighty-six. The quilting pattern in this example of
her work is a circle of eight roses with borders of twist and
running feather. 6 ft 8 in × 7 ft 4 in (203 cm × 224 cm).
(Beamish North of England Open Air Museum)

producing textiles in Wales and parts of Scotland, and about the workshops of such craft specialists as the village blacksmith, wheelwright, wood turner, and basketmaker.

The Bureau's involvement with quilting was actively supported by the Women's Institutes and one of the first functions undertaken by the Bureau was the setting up of a register of craft workers. By 1929 the Bureau had a register of 170 quilters in County Durham and South Wales who wanted orders for work. Indeed, the work done on behalf of the quilters was considered one of the most successful endeavours undertaken by the Bureau. In a report which covered the years 1929 to 1936, it was explained that, since the Bureau was not constituted to give money, a grant of £250 had been sought from the Pilgrim Trust for the purpose of buying materials and establishing classes for the training of young women by the older quilters.

Success was immediate and during the period of greatest distress whole families were saved from utter destruction by the income derived from the sale of the work of their womenfolk.

Two factors in this success were the high aesthetic quality of the designs, and the provision of a capital sum for which no return was demanded.[12]

The first exhibition of Welsh and Durham quilting was held in London in 1928 and it brought in enough orders to keep the quilters busy for some months. In fact, the Bureau reported that in the first three years of quilting sales and exhibitions, over £10,000 had been earned. (An officer of the Bureau was responsible for controlling the rates of pay, liaising with the quilters, providing materials, etc.)

The classes initiated by the Bureau to train new quilters and generally to raise the standard of the craft were also successful – six were started in Wales alone – and quilts were marketed through London retailers. Quilters were paid by the square foot for their work – one shilling and sixpence ($7\frac{1}{2}$p) per square foot, and a quilter making a double-bed quilt would earn about £3 16s (£3.80p). The price subsequently was increased to two shillings (10p) a square foot and half a crown ($12\frac{1}{2}$p) for very fine work. The Bureau concluded that although organizing the quilters had been 'an emergency expedient', there was no reason why the sale of quilts should not remain a permanent industry.[13]

A pamphlet issued by the Bureau in 1937 further emphasized the Bureau's belief in this small home industry: 'Quilting is not a revival or a part of the antique trade, it is the last traditional needlework left in the country.'[14] Alas, the Bureau's report of 1939–47 had no mention of the quilters whatsoever. By this time World War II had intervened, there was a shortage of materials, and the women themselves were occupied in more profitable employment.

PATTERNS

Prior to the establishment of the Rural Industries Bureau, the Agricultural Economics Research Institute in Oxford had conducted a survey into the economic and social position of rural industries. One of the many facts revealed in the survey was that quilters in the north of England and South Wales were using designs dating from the time of Queen Elizabeth I: the wives of the miners were following in both technique and pattern a tradition that was over 300 years old. The designs themselves, stated the report – especially designs like feathers, bellows and the beehive – showed that inspiration came from the simple things in nature and domesticity.

Quilting designs and their origins are a subject which many people have attempted to investigate. Elizabeth Hake, who published the results of her research in 1937, wrote with 'a measure of confidence' that Welsh quilting patterns could be identified by their geometrical character; those of the north of England by a freer and more flowing tendency; and those of Wessex because they were

chiefly floral in content.[15] She also referred to superstition in quilting – the inclusion of hearts in a wedding quilt and the undesirability of breaking a cable design in the border in the belief that a broken cable invited the risk of a life cut short by disaster. Quilters themselves will tell you that a broken cable could have a much less sinister implication – that an inexperienced needlewoman had been incapable of drawing and working the cable around the quilt's corners!

Mavis Fitzrandolph, who helped research rural industries for the Agricultural Economics Research Institute in the early 1920s, was involved with a number of publications about rural industries including a book on quilting. She stated that Welsh quilters, at least at the beginning of the present century, were partial to patterns with a centrepiece and one or more borders enclosed in rectangular frames, and that the strip quilts of the north of England often featured the running feather, the twist, chain, plait and bellows.

One of the difficulties of trying to attribute any

Above: The leaf, spiral and Tudor rose, designs typical of Glamorganshire, were used by the Porth Quilters in this 1933 quilting design. The quilt was made in beige cotton poplin and filled with sheep's wool. 6 ft 2 in × 5 ft 10 in (188 cm × 178 cm). (Photograph courtesy of the Welsh Folk Museum)

Left: Quilting pattern used in an 1888 Welsh marriage quilt made by Mary Williams of Pontypridd. A heart is enclosed in a circular fan surrounded by quarter fans. The quilt was made in white sateen and backed with a floral print. 7 ft 2 in × 7 ft 8 in (218 cm × 234 cm). (Photograph courtesy of the Welsh Folk Museum)

pattern regionally or historically is the fact that many quilters jealously guarded their templates, having made them from their own drawings and often handing them down from mother to daughter. A number of household items were used to help with the marking – wineglass was one of the favourite background fillings along with the diamond; the latter could be marked with a chalked string which was stretched and then snapped on top of the material. Another favourite background pattern was the overlapping half circle, which as a patchwork pattern was called shell, and as a quilting pattern sometimes 'scale' and 'mother of thousands'. Templates for marking were made from either cardboard or paper: shapes were generally basic and much of the fill-in was freehand. An article

in *The Embroideress* of 1927 showed a magnificent set of hexagonal, circular and elliptical templates made in mahogany, with tiny knobs to facilitate handling; the hexagons were used for patchwork. Such grand templates would not be found in the sewing-box of the average quilter.

Shells were frequently used as a quilting pattern also, especially by quilters who lived in coastal towns. Fans were another favourite, and throughout both Durham and Northumberland the feather and the rose were popular.[16] Both the lover's knot and the heart were used for marriage quilts – the detail on page 26 shows an example of the former. One wedding quilt in the collection of the Welsh Folk Museum, made about 1886 by Miss Mary Williams of Glamorgan, has a central design of a heart enclosed in a circular fan. Tulips set in leaves are in the four corners of the central area together with six Paisley motifs – the Paisley seed pod is called the 'Welsh Pear'. Both the tulips and the pear are also designs found carved in Welsh love-spoons.[17]

The extent to which nature inspired design is evident in the frequent use of flowers and leaves. The earliest dated quilt in the collection of the Welsh Folk Museum – made in 1840 in Pembrokeshire – has a central motif of rosettes, buds and spirals enclosed by a border of twisted rope. There are large beech leaves in the corners of the central rectangle, with curved leaves, thistles and pine cones distributed in the two borders.[18] Patterns also came from other sources: one lady, a Mrs M.E. Shepherd of Northumberland, made her patterns from paper doilies and the emblem on the family Bible. Her children remember that she was given to drawing patterns in the salt dish while sitting at the dinner table.[19]

Strip quilts in Turkey Red and white were a traditional combination in both Durham and Northumberland and obviously one which had

certain advantages. It was far easier to work patterns in long continuous strips than to deal with a central motif; and one strip could be marked at a time as the quilt was unrolled in the frame. A number of continuous patterns were used on the strip quilts – even one called the Lambton Worm (a pair of wavy lines with a lozenge infill) which took its name from a legendary reptilian monster in County Durham. The quilt on page 27 shows the conventional form of the strip quilt, though in this case the quilting has been done from the opposite side, a white whole cloth ground which would be considered the top. Strip quilts were also made in Wales, though often in wool and in different colour combinations. And in the Isle of Man the striped tops were made in two colours – dark blue, red, and black or green being the preferred choices: the last named was popular because greenweed, the dye source, was extensively grown in local fields. One quilt in the collection of the Manx Museum, dating from 1840, is red and black striped, with an overall diamond pattern; another is blue linen and red wool.[20]

The strip quilt and the whole cloth quilt were the preferred 'canvas' on which most quilters of Wales, Durham and Northumberland chose to work. Quilting, in their minds, was a much higher art than piecing, and although they changed their ideas about colour and cloth – going from white cotton to sateen and pastels in the early twentieth century – they stayed true to the original format. One of the curious sidetracks they did follow, however, was the quilting of prints – especially the large cotton squares that had been printed to resemble Paisley shawls. These usually appeared with the Paisley design round the border of a plain centre. They were an ideal background on which to display the quilter's art, especially when she chose an elaborate pattern which had a central design. Prints were also used to make whole cloth quilts, though obviously these were never as successful since they did nothing to enhance the quilting designs.

Detail of quilted lovers' knot sur-rounded by wine-glass quilting.

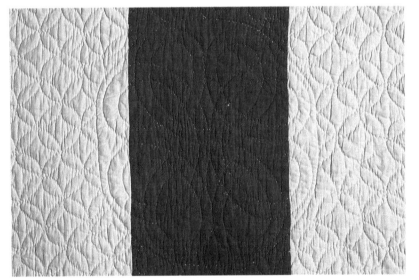

FRAMES AND FILLINGS

Three layers of cloth stitched together was called wadded quilting in the north of England and 'hard quilting' in the west. One of the most troublesome types of filling found in British quilts (but preferred for its softness) was lamb's wool – troublesome because it was usually collected from the hedgerows and then had to be thoroughly scoured before it could be used. Mrs Elizabeth Hake's book records the details of such enterprise in the north of

England in the nineteenth century. Two pounds of wool were needed to fill a large quilt, and before the wool could be carded with wire brushes, it had to be washed in soapy water, rinsed several times and then dried out of doors on a breezy day – usually spread on the ground under a fishnet to keep it from blowing away. A certain amount of natural oil was left in the wool on purpose, since it was believed that this was a safeguard against moths.

Late nineteenth-century Turkey Red and white cotton strip quilt with white cotton backing, probably made as a marriage quilt since the central quilting pattern is a lovers' knot. The top of this quilt was probably the whole cloth side since the pattern was worked without regard to the strips. 6 ft 5 in × 6 ft 6 in (196 cm × 198 cm). (Beamish North of England Open Air Museum)

Pieced green and white cotton star quilt with zig-zag border
made at Pity Me, County Durham, about 1880. Quilted with
roses and diamonds. 7 ft 3 in × 7 ft 5 in (221 cm × 226 cm).
(Beamish North of England Open Air Museum)

The practice of using lamb's wool as a filling is also a matter of record in the Scottish Borders in the early twentieth century, and during World War II it experienced something of a revival due to the scarcity of other materials. In Scotland, where the details of the procedure are still a matter of personal experience, quilt cases were made in butter-muslin which had quilting lines marked with an indelible pen. The designs were functional in comparison to the fine quilting of Durham and Northumberland. Each section of the quilt was stuffed as the sewing was completed, and considerably more wool was used than in the other example described above.

Wool was used as a wadding in Wales as well. In parts of Cornwall, if silk was being used, then often a layer of butter-muslin was added between the layer of silk and lamb's wool. This practice applied in particular to silk skirts, which in 1860 cost one guinea (£1.05p) to be quilted by a professional.

The use of worn blankets seemed universal especially in utilitarian quilts in Ireland, England and Scotland – in Ireland there is evidence that worn woollen clothing was used in its entirety as quilt filling.[21] It can be said with some certainty, in fact, that just about any material was considered as possible wadding through the years – flannel, down, frayed woollens cut into tiny scraps and mixed with

paper – as well as the more costly mechanically-prepared cotton wool and domette, a manufactured woollen lining material which was often used with silk. And, of course, old worn quilts were recycled with the addition of a new cover and backing.

The type of frame that seemed most universally used consisted of only four pieces of wood – two lengthy bars to which webbing had been nailed to attach the quilt, and two cross pieces, called 'swords' in the north of England, which fitted through slits in the bars. Each sword had a number of holes and the bars were kept in place with wooden pegs. The methods of attaching the quilt to the frame, however, seem to vary slightly. In County Tyrone in both the nineteenth and early twentieth centuries, quilters obviously worked from one side to the other instead of starting from the middle. All three thicknesses of fabric were basted together at one end and this end was attached to one bar. Only the backing, however, was attached to the opposite bar and kept firmly rolled. The filling and top layer were kept loose and held in place as the work progressed. In the north of England, the procedure during the same period seems slightly different in that the backing was first attached to both bars, then the wadding and top layer added, with all three thicknesses being rolled at once, from

Centre of Welsh cotton print whole cloth quilt filled with lamb's wool. Prints were used frequently despite the fact that they did not enhance the quilting. Made near Swansea about 1910. 6 ft 2 in × 7 ft (188 cm × 213 cm). (Jen Jones)

Right: Centre of pink cotton sateen quilt made in Swansea about 1910. The quilting, in red thread, features a star, snails, leaves and diamonds. 6 ft 6 in × 6 ft 11 in (198 cm × 211 cm). (Jeñ Jones)

Far right: Green cotton sateen backed with pink sateen and quilted with pink thread. Made in Wales about 1900. 6 ft 7 in × 6 ft 9 in (201 cm × 206 cm). (Jen Jones)

one side. Quilts with central designs, of course, required to be started from the middle.

Marking was done in two ways: either the top was completely marked being attached to the frame, usually with blue pencil, or, if the quilt was to be worked from side to side, the marking was done as the work progressed. One of the more unusual ways of marking in the north of England – a method which is still used today – was with a needle, which was drawn lightly around the edge of the template. The old term for this method of quilting was 'handlaid'. The method itself was best achieved with the needle stuck in a cork and the end slightly blunted – one North Country quilter who still works today uses a dulled carpenter's awl for the same purpose. Needle-marking is especially suitable for satins, for a needle line can easily perforate the outer surface. The method does not, however, allow for any mistakes in drawing on the part of the marker.

Although marking with a needle or pen was a favourite method used in the North Country, marking with an iron was also recommended. S.F.A. Caulfield's *Dictionary of Needlework*, published in 1887, gave precise instructions for marking when quilting by hand. The material was to be folded at the cross, ironed down, then folded and ironed again with the aid of a paper strip for measuring the widths. Once all the lines had been ironed, the material was to be turned and the cross lines ironed in. This method, of course, produced the checked diamond background – any quilting pattern with a curve would require another method of marking.

A SOCIABLE ACTIVITY

Quilting was traditionally a good excuse for socializing – and not only in connection with the type of fund-raising projects associated with the Chapel Quilt Clubs mentioned earlier. At least six women could sit around the frame at a time and it was customary to keep children busy threading the needles – this was considered a girl's introduction to quilting. In Ireland in the nineteenth and early twentieth centuries, the 'Quilting' was regarded as a big night and the opportunity for entertainment and courting. Quilting parties were also known to have been held in Yorkshire in the nineteenth century. The traditional tipple on these occasions was a cold posset consisting of new milk, sugar, currants and rum or beer.[22] In the Scottish Borders, women gathered to quilt in the evenings because they were otherwise occupied during the day. Not only did they gossip, they recited poetry to each other while they worked. In Wales, the quilting party is not recorded as a tradition – rather the members of a household, helped by the local quilting professional, if there was one, handled all the necessary quiltmaking, even if a number of quilts were required for an upcoming wedding.

An insight into the quilting party as a tradition is best illustrated through a few verses by Pat McCarty, a farmer in Antrim and social commentator of the nineteenth century, who wrote a poem called 'The Quiltin'. A quilting party in his part of the world was organized only after a quilt top had been pieced from scraps and had grown big enough to be considered 'clever'. (This meant that the pieced top was of generous proportions and not 'skimpit' – the opposite of 'clever'.) The pieced top was then stretched on a frame, with its backing and blanket filling, and the frame set up in either the kitchen or barn. The girls arrived for the quilting first and in a few hours completed their zig-zag or crossed diagonal quilting – finishing before the men arrived. When the last stitch was finished, the floor was cleared and the games and dancing began. Currant buns and tea were served and also a supper which sometimes included blancmange. The evening was one of general merriment and most of McCarty's poem records the entertainment and the music from a piano. These four verses give an impression:

It was the bonnie quiltin' that, in Mrs Gibson's barn,
A nicht to be remember'd lang in annals o' the glen.
The notice gi'en a week afore to whom it micht
    consarn
Had brocht the purty lassies oot, and lassies bring the
    men.

Wee Meg had come, — 'deed half the glen, a score o'
    girls at laste,
And fifteen stone o' Alice Hill, the sweetest lassie
    there.
It needs a yard or mair o' airm to gang aroon' her
    waist,
But what's circumference to love? A figure, naethin'
    mair.

And while the lassies sew'd their seam the men stood
    roon' the wa',
And jok'd and laugh'd wi' narvous glee, and turnit in
    their taes,
And thocht aboot the dance to come wi' fears that
    werena sma',
And wore the air o' men that ken they wear their
    Sunday claes . . .

O 'twas the famous quiltin', that, in Mrs Gibson's
    barn,
And folk that liv'd a distance aff, awa', far up the
    glen,
It's true as true, a sartin fact, and nae bit rhymer's
    yarn,
They werena in their beds that nicht till nearly half-
    past ten.[23]

Notes

1. Therle Hughes, *English Domestic Needlework 1660-1860*, London, 1961.
2. Letter to William Drennan, No. 848, 12 May 1800, Public Record Office, Belfast.
3. Catalogue, SWRI Exhibition of Needlework, Royal Scottish Academy, 1934.
4. M.S. Lockwood, *Art Embroidery*, London, 1878, p.53.
5. E. Glaister, *Needlework*, London, 1880, p.97.
6. Mrs Archibald Christie, *Embroidery*, London, 1909, p.148.
7. David Minter (ed.), *Modern Needlecraft*, London, 1933, p.44.
8. Hughes, op.cit.
9. Mavis Fitzrandolph, *Traditional Quilting*, London, 1954.
10. Laura Jones, 'Quilting', *Ulster Folk Life*, 1975.
11. *North Country Lore and Legend*, Newcastle, 1887, p.224.
12. *Report on the Work of the Rural Industries Bureau 1929-36*, London: Rural Industries Bureau, 1936, p.16.
13. Ibid.
14. *The Rural Industries of England, Scotland and Wales*, London: Rural Industries Bureau, 1937, p.12.
15. Elizabeth Hake, *English Quilting Old and New*, London, 1937.
16. Tyne and Wear County Council, Museums Information Sheet, n.d.
17. Ilid E. Anthony, 'Quilting and Patchwork in Wales', *Amgueddfa*, Winter 1972.
18. Ibid.
19. Tyne and Wear County Council, op.cit.
20. Larch S. Garrad, 'Quilting and Patchwork in the Isle of Man', *Folk Life*, Vol. 17, 1979.
21. Deirdre E. Morton, 'Quilting in Glenlark, Co. Tyrone', *Ulster Folk Life*, Vol. 5, 1959.
22. Anne Ward, 'Quilting in the North of England', *Folk Life*, Vol. 4, 1966.
23. J. Stevenson, *Pat McCarty: His Rhymes With a Setting*, London: Edward Arnold, 1903, p.79.

2

COTTON AND WOOL

Silk, wool, linen and cotton are all ancient fibres which quiltmakers have used in pursuit of their craft. Wool has its own special niche in the history of British quilts, but regettably wool does not endure and to some extent much of our knowledge about its use in quilts must be based on supposition.

Cotton first appeared in Britain as a possible textile for quilts about 1600. It is mentioned in a petition now in the London and Guildhall Library:

. . . diverse people in this Kingdome, but chiefly in the countie of Lancashire, have found out the trade of making of other Fustians, made of a kind of Bombast, or Downe, being a fruit of the earth growing upon little

Portrait of Queen Caroline

shrubs or bushes, brought into this Kingdome by the Turkey merchants, from Smyrna, Cyprus . . . commonly called cotton wool . . . There is at the least 40 thousand pieces of Fustian of this kind yearly made in England . . . and thousands of poor people set on working of these Fustians.[1]

The use of cotton in making fustian – a cloth with a linen warp and cotton weft – was a well-established practice by the mid-seventeenth century in the Manchester area. Much of the linen used in the process came from Scotland, where flax was grown, and where linen-weaving was an established industry. Following the Union of Parliaments in 1707, when more markets were opened to the Scots, the west of Scotland became a major textile exporting centre, sending great quantities of linen to America and the West Indies, as well as 'a stuff cross-striped with yellow, red, and other mixtures' and striped muslins.[2] Flax was also a major crop in Ireland, and linen was so popular a material for costume that in the sixteenth century Henry VIII passed a law which forbade Irishmen from using more than seven yards of linen in the making of a shirt. The growth of the cotton industry in Britain was spurred by the invention of the spinning jenny by James Hargreaves about 1765, making possible the spinning of eight to eleven threads simultaneously, and the spinning frame by Richard Arkwright in 1769, which further mechanized and improved the manufacturing process. The cotton industry grew in Lancashire and by the end of the eighteenth century it was also flourishing around Glasgow, where the manufacture of cotton and cotton thread, as well as the subsidiary industries of printing and dyeing, were well-entrenched.

Cotton printing in Britain in the seventeenth century was greatly influenced by the exotic floral

Pieced scrap quilt with printed portrait titled 'Her Most
Gracious Majesty, Queen Caroline of England'. Wool filled
and linen backed and quilted with a central star, spirals,
waves and flowers. Made in 1810. 7 ft 10 in × 8 ft 8 in
(239 cm × 264 cm). (Photograph courtesy of the Welsh Folk
Museum)

designs which the East India Company had begun importing after 1600. The popularity of these chintzes gave a particular impetus to certain forms of appliqué, which are discussed in Chapter 4. The fashionable craze for the cottons arriving from the East also encouraged experiments in cotton dyeing in Britain in an attempt to find mordants for fixing. The first British imitations of the eastern chintzes had used wax-resist and woodblock printing for outlines and handfill for colours, none of which had proved satisfactory. By the 1670s, however, the technique of using wooden blocks, sometimes with metal inserts for printing, had been combined with successful experiments in mordants and the industry was thriving.

Initially, most of the cotton printers appeared in south-eastern England. The invention of the first successful rotary printing machine by Thomas Bell, a Scot, in 1783, plus the fact that most of the all-cotton cloth industry was developing around Lancashire, eventually saw the removal of the printing function from the capital to the north, where it became centred on Lancashire and Carlisle.

SCRAPS OF HISTORY

A very elementary knowledge of textile manufacturing in the UK is helpful to the quilt historian, if only because it places certain quilts in context. Linen, for example, which today would be considered costly and perhaps too heavy to work, was once manufactured extensively in Scotland and Ireland. In Scotland, it was usually quite coarse in texture because of the quality of the flax, and finer linen had to be imported. None the less, linen was readily available and more accessible to quiltmakers than cotton. Damask, another Irish speciality, was also considered at one time an inexpensive cloth for a bed covering – a very rough utility quilt made of cut-up damask table cloths is in the collection of the Ulster Folk and Transport Museum. The woven Paisley shawls, which nowadays fetch such high prices in the auction rooms, were so plentiful and cheap in the nineteenth century that they were used as backing for a quilt: sometimes they were even used as the top and heavily quilted. The prized Indian chintzes, on the other hand, which started coming into the country in the seventeenth century, could be used only sparingly.

Costume also affected the quiltmaker's art in that scraps from the fashionable prints and colours used in dressmaking often ended up in the sewing-basket for use in piecing quilt tops. This is one reason why scrap quilts often provide such an interesting insight into period costume – and sometimes cause confusion in attempts at dating. Quilts that include machine stitching (often only to finish the edges instead of the traditional two parallel lines of a running stitch) date after 1856 when Isaac Merrit Singer opened his first agency in Glasgow to sell the new sewing machine. Even so, sewing machines were not widely available in Britain until the 1860s. It is less easy to attempt quilt dating by examining the prints used, since scraps may have been accumulated over a long period of time, and often the piecing itself was a leisurely project. Even when one can date a certain type of print, this in itself is no clue to when the quilt was made. The scrap quilt on page 38 is a good example. The large squares of commemorative print in the outside border bear cameo portraits of Queen Victoria and the date 1887, the year of her golden jubilee. The cottons used on the inside of the quilt, however, are much older, so one may surmise that the pieces had been collected over a long period and that the commemorative print was added close to the quilt's completion. A good nineteenth-century scrap quilt, nevertheless, is as good as any collection of old sample books for charting the fashionable changes in costume textiles and it has to be enjoyed for that reason.

Printed cottons used in quilts can also provide something of a social document, especially if, as in the case of the star quilt on page 35, one knows that the cottons were off-cuts from an Irish shirt factory in Londonderry. Off-cuts could be bought from the factory for 2s 6d (12½p) a bag in the 1920s but the factory girls were often given leftover squares – the squares of cotton normally used to fashion side vents in the shirts. Mrs Hawkins, who made this shirt quilt in 1923, worked in the factory by day, and by night sat at her treadle sewing machine stitching the two-inch squares into various patterns. It is machine stitched, without wadding, and it has a patched back. Mrs Hawkins made each of her four daughters a shirt quilt when they married. Some of these quilts were backed with flour bags, a popular practice, the bags being purchased from the baker at 6d (2½p) each, then scrubbed with paraffin oil to remove the blue lettering. After sitting for a few days, the bags were then boiled in soda and soap

Mary Hawkins of Londonderry, Ireland, a seamstress in a
shirt factory, pieced this star quilt in 1923. It is entirely
machine sewn and has no wadding or quilting. The back is
patched. 6 ft 2 in × 4 ft 11 in (188 cm × 150 cm). (Ulster Folk
and Transport Museum)

Pieced scrap quilt made in Llandeilo, Wales, about 1885.
Filled with lamb's wool and quilted with a sunburst centre.
6 ft 10 in × 7 ft 1 in (208 cm × 216 cm). (Jen Jones)

This scrap quilt of squares and rectangles was made about
1910 in Dryswlyn, Wales. It has no filling but has been
quilted in waves and circles. 5 ft 8 in × 6 ft 11 in (173 cm ×
211 cm). (Jen Jones)

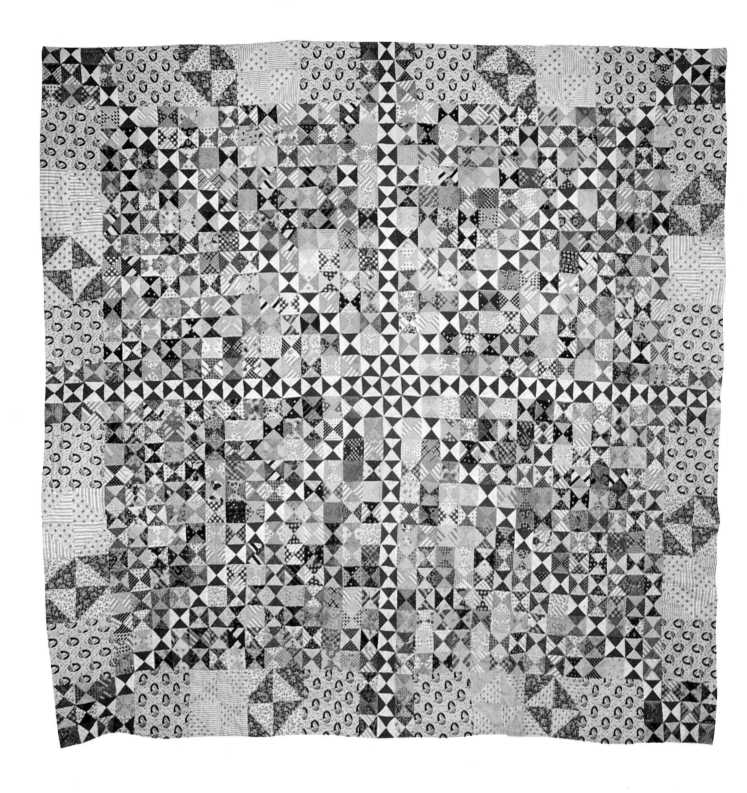

Scrap quilt from the Lake District of England. The triangles, pieced from dress fabrics, have been highlighted by Turkey Red and white cotton crosses. The quilt is filled and has a linen backing. The quilting pattern is wineglass and shell. Made in 1887. 7 ft 9 in × 8 ft 1 in (236 cm × 246 cm). (Author's collection)

powder until all the lettering had disappeared and the cotton was considered clean enough to be used.

Another quilt, possibly made from off-cuts from a Scottish shirt factory, is in the collection of Glasgow Museums and Art Galleries. It is made in a Log Cabin Pattern and dates from the second half of the nineteenth century. Aside from its possible connection with the clothing industry of the time it provides another kind of social clue – hand-crocheted edging along one side indicates that the quilt was made for a traditional box bed. A Log Cabin quilt made of shirting cottons, also from Scotland and dating from about 1860, is in the collection of the Bowes Museum at Barnard Castle, County Durham. It has a heavily patched back in squares and rectangles which in its own way is as interesting as the front.

Cottons with small print designs, often on a white ground, as opposed to the flamboyant imitations of Indian chintzes, were not only used for shirts but of course were used in ladies' gowns. The advent of roller printing saw the production of a number of single colour prints, often arranged as stripes, in the early part of the nineteenth century. Previously there had been a preference for dark grounds with rich floral patterns, followed by an extensive use of drab colours like olive green. By the 1830s, the wider use of Turkey Red dyes, combined with blue

This cameo portrait of Queen Victoria, found in one of the fabrics used in the border of the scrap quilt opposite, is a commemorative print issued to celebrate the Queen's golden jubilee in 1887.

Detail of pieced and appliquéd white cotton coverlet. Made about 1810 from a variety of dress cottons. 8 ft 5 in × 9 ft 2 in (257 cm × 279 cm). (The Castle Museum, York)

Woven Paisley shawl which has been made into a quilt. It is filled with a blanket and backed with burgundy sateen. Made near Cardigan, Wales, in the late nineteenth century. 5 ft 10 in × 7 ft 1 in (178 cm × 216 cm). (Jen Jones)

A variety of scrap bag dress cottons and shirtings have been used in this Suffolk puffs scrap quilt made in 1890. Each puff measures one-half inch across (15 mm). 7 ft 1 in × 5 ft 10 in (216 cm × 178 cm). (The Castle Museum, York)

and yellow, had become fashionable for prints used for costume, and by 1840 the emphasis had returned to light backgrounds and delicate floral patterns. From 1860 onwards, the cotton print

gown was usually associated with working-class women and servants: middle-class women were turning their attentions towards more luxurious textiles for their adornment.

UTILITY WOOL

Wool quilts have a special place in the history of quiltmaking, though time and the ravaging moth have taken their toll. The weaving of wool cloth itself is a very ancient craft in Britain, and from early times wool coverings of one description or another were used on beds. Many were crude. The 'cloutie' quilt, which consisted of a weft of thin strips of old stuff woven on a cotton warp, was known in the Scottish Highlands and elsewhere: it was often made by old and infirm weavers who had lost the facility for finer work.

Early wool quilts were utilitarian and made without much thought for colour or design. Odd bits of leftover wool from the loom or from worn-out clothing were simply sewn together until an adequate rectangle – enough to cover a bed – was

achieved. Many of these covers, none the less, possessed a modest charm. Despite appearances they did provide warmth, and the humble covering served many an emigrant. The Scots weavers who went out to Upper Canada in the middle of the nineteenth century, for example, were prompted by the severe climatic conditions to continue making these utility covers, and the homespun quilt became an established tradition in their new life. The 'Hit and Miss' pattern, a collection of different-sized squares and rectangles sewn into strips, was an obvious choice of pattern for these wool covers, since it utilized leftover ends from the loom. Descendants of Hebridean Scots who emigrated to Quebec in the last century still had vivid memories of the type of utility covers made by their mothers:

Navy and red woollen twill pieced in windmill blades
pattern. Blanket filled and edged with blue braid. Red
Paisley print backing. Made in Northern Ireland in the
nineteenth century. 7 ft 10 in × 6 ft 2 in (239 cm × 188 cm).
(Ulster Folk and Transport Museum)

'It was just odds and ends of your dresses and aprons, and so on . . . they never had material enough of one kind, like. Just hit and miss . . . and tacks . . . instead of quilting them, they were tacked . . .' (Christie MacKenzie).[3]

Other designs used by these Hebridean women in Canada also utilized the scrap-bag – Log Cabin and crazy piecing. In other parts of Canada, and at a time when larger pieces of hand-woven wool were available, another type of pattern became popular with Scots settlers – a pattern reminiscent of the simple geometric shapes commonly used in Amish quilts. The patterns were large and few – a square, diamond or rectangle, surrounded by two borders – and the quilting was entirely functional. These simple quilt designs were also used frequently by Welsh quilters, although in their hands the quilting was more of an accomplishment.

Above left: Whole cloth woollen quilt, one side in red, the other in green. Quilted with flowers and leaves. Made in Wales in 1875. 5 ft 8 in × 6 ft 7 in (173 cm × 201 cm). (Jen Jones)

Below left: Detail showing the flower shapes used by Scott.

The carding, spinning and weaving of wool also thrived as a cottage industry in Wales in the seventeenth and eighteenth centuries, and Welsh flannel in particular became known internationally. Whole families worked at the business in their leisure time, in order to satisfy their own domestic requirements and to sell the surplus to dealers who carried woollens on pack horses to markets in England.

Most of the Welsh antique woollen quilts that survive date from the nineteenth century and they show several distinct preferences for pattern. These are the strip quilt, the whole cloth quilt, and the quilt with a single large geometric shape in the centre, like a diamond or turned square. Depending on the ability of the maker, the quilting on these covers ranges from medium to fine.

Wool quilts were also a tradition in the Isle of Man. The Manx Museum has a number of woollen quilts in its collection, half of which can be termed whole cloth quilts – two lengths of cloth with an interlining which have been quilted together. One of these, created in Kirk Arbory in the 1830s, is made of salmon red linsey-wolsey with a wineglass and diamond quilting pattern.[4] In Ireland, too, the wool quilt – red flannel whole cloth – was known, sometimes made with patterned quilting. Women who were practising economy in Ireland, however, were known to dye old blankets red and then quilt two together.

Wool was also used for piecing, although admittedly it was not an easy textile to work when designs called for small patches. Examples of wool patchwork quilts are few: the red and navy woollen twill quilt in a windmill pattern on page 41 is a graphic example of how effective woollen cloth could be when used in a simple design. Many of the wool quilts that have survived are known to have been made by tailors. Sample-books of suitings were an obvious source of textile supply, and often these samples were just machined together for a quick utility cover. In Ireland, these squares were also crocheted together with red wool – the Ulster Folk and Transport Museum has several examples of this type of work. The quilt on page 43 was made by Walter Scott, a master tailor from Crookham in Northumberland. It is an unusual combination of machine appliqué – no edges are turned – and a medallion centre made of uniform cloth. It is said

Walter Scott, a master tailor from Crookham, Northumberland, began this piece of machine appliqué in 1872, using off-cuts from the suits he was tailoring. 6 ft 8 in × 7 ft (203 cm × 213 cm). (Beamish North of England Open Air Museum)

Pieced woollen quilt with red flannel diamond centre.
Roughly quilted with black thread in diamonds and circles
and filled with lamb's wool. Made in Wales in 1890. 5 ft 5 in
× 6 ft 1 in (165 cm × 185 cm). (Jen Jones)

Quilt of woollen suitings, using squares, rectangles and
diamonds backed with floral print and made by Mrs
Elizabeth McGill of Mourne, County Down, in 1935. 6ft
3in×6ft 5in (190cm×197cm). (Ulster Folk and Transport
Museum)

Pieced top made in Scotland during the Depression in the
1930s. Fabrics used include tartan, cotton, canvas and
flannel. 5 ft 3 in × 5 ft 5 in (160 cm × 165 cm). (Author's
collection)

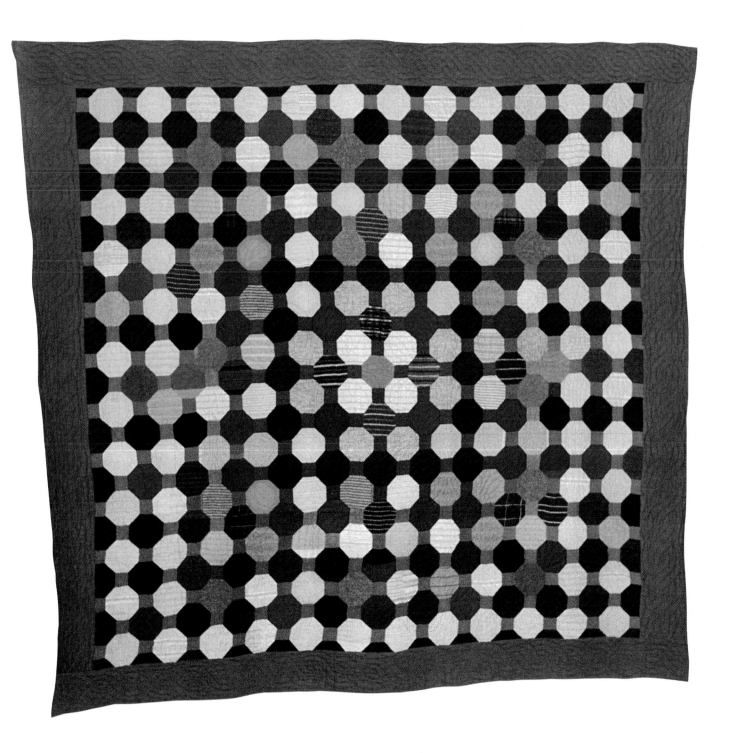

The multi-coloured flannels and suitings in this quilt of octagons were purchased as remnants from Scottish drapers, who travelled the Northumberland countryside. The quilt, made by Mrs Sybil Heslop, who lived at Ovington West Farm, is pieced on both sides and quilted in a wineglass pattern. Mrs Heslop was eighty-five years of age when she died in 1913. 7 ft × 7 ft 4 in (213 cm × 224 cm). (Beamish North of England Open Air Museum)

This photograph of a travelling pedlar or 'Scotch Draper' trading in the countryside was taken in 1855 by James Johnston, a Scottish photographer. (Scottish National Portrait Gallery)

that he started the project as a small cover but then just carried on, using off-cuts from the suits he was tailoring.

Buying fabric was not easy in eighteenth- and nineteenth-century Britain, especially for women who lived in rural communities. The tradesman whom many depended on was the pedlar, a very familiar figure on the main roads in the country. The pedlar had a variety of names, such as the tallyman, the Scotchman (also the chapman in Scotland) or the Manchesterman. Whatever his origins, he was the link between the mills of Wales, Scotland, Ireland and Lancashire and the consumer, and he moved about the country with his packs full of flannel, linen and cotton. Sometimes he would set up temporarily in a market place in one of the larger towns; other times he would simply call on individual farms and cottages. The cloth pedlar is

still a tradesman within living memory. The quilt made by Mrs Sybil Heslop, on page 47, is made of different-coloured flannels and suitings, bought from such a pedlar, a 'Scotch draper', at the turn of this century during his visits to farmhouses in Northumberland.

Wool continued to be used in utility covers right through the Depression years of the twentieth century, when economy again became important and all types of worn clothing and scraps were used in the making of bed-covers. The unfinished pieced top on page 46, made in Scotland, has a mix of flannel, worn tartan, cotton and even canvas interfacing. Another quilt of the same era – made in Ireland by Mrs McGill, an indefatigable quiltmaker – is pictured on page 45. It is also made of squares, rectangles and diamonds in a mix of woollen and suiting fabrics.

TURKEY RED

The study of dyes and their application to cloth is one which requires much enquiry and an exhaustive knowledge of the transition from dyeing with vegetable matter to dyeing with chemicals. The appearance of certain colours at certain periods in time depended not only on fashion but on

the cloth trade's contemporary knowledge of dyeing techniques.

In the eighteenth century, the English chintz printers, who were working with wooden blocks and printing by hand, used madder for reds, browns and purples, indigo for blue and weld for yellow. In

Sailor's quilt, made from books of cotton samples which include Turkey Red prints. Nicholas White of Dundee, a steward in the whaling ships, *Balaena* and *Terra Nova,* made this quilt in the late nineteenth century. Over 100 different prints have been used, including line checks in twenty different colourways and thirty-five varieties of stripes. White used a variety of squares, rectangles and triangles (including Flying Geese) for his masterpiece and quilted it roughly in waves. White, who made the quilt while serving in the *Balaena,* died in 1897 at the age of fifty-nine and is buried at Yell, Shetland. 7 ft 6 in × 7 ft 9 in (229 cm × 236 cm). (City of Dundee Museums and Art Galleries)

Detail of Turkey Red Paisley print used in Welsh quilt about 1900. The familiar Paisley seed pod is printed with blue and yellow peaches. Wave quilted and un-filled. 6 ft 3 in × 7 ft 3 in (191 cm × 221 cm). (Jen Jones)

the latter part of the century, Quercitron bark was also used for yellow. The outstanding development in dyeing techniques which captured the imagination of quiltmakers and influenced quilt design in particular (also, of course, costume) was the discovery of the process for dyeing the non-bleeding Turkey Red. Turkey Red in both whole cloth quilts and red and white strip quilts became commonplace from the mid-nineteenth century as a suitable background for the quilting skills exercised in the mining communities of the north of England. The Irish favoured Turkey Red for appliqué, using it on a white ground, and many nineteenth-century stitchery writers also took to recommending it as a suitable colour for various types of patchwork piecing. Turkey Red Paisley prints were also popular with Welsh quilters at the end of the nineteenth century (see above) even though they proved very unsuitable as a quilting 'ground': the stitches did not show through the print.

The secret of producing 'Adrianople Red' had originated in the East and been known to dyers in continental Europe for some time, but it was not until the latter part of the eighteenth century that it became available in Britain. A Lancashire man, John Wilson, had sent a young man to Turkey in 1753 to discover the secret of Turkey Red dye. Wilson, however, was unhappy with the results and pursued the matter no further. It was more than thirty years before someone else picked up the gauntlet. The public was informed that the

technique was available in an advertisement in the *Glasgow Mercury* of 15 December 1785:

Dale and Macintosh have now got their Dyehouse finished, and are just begun to dye cotton yarn Turkey Red for the Manufacturers at large, at 3s per lb weight.

The excellency of this colour is already known here, as it has been tried and found to stand the process of bleaching, when woven along with green linen, or cotton yarn without impairing, but rather increasing its beauty and lustre.

The yarn is received in by Mr M'Donald at Messrs. Macintosh and Murdoch's warehouse, in Trongate in quantities not less than 60 lbs at one time from one person.

The Manufacturers will please to loose the heering bands, and tie them slack, in order to receive the colour equally; and put up the cotton in hanks, from 4 to 6 oz each with a strong string. Each customer will get a particular mark to put on these strings which they will please to keep and use always for that purpose.

To accommodate the Manufacturers in general, Mr Dale will keep an assortment of this dyed cotton at his warehouses which he will sell, with the addition of 3s per lb for the dyeing to the original price.

The distinction of introducing Turkey Red to Glasgow's expanding cotton industry (the first cotton spinning mill in Scotland had been erected in Rothesay in 1778) belonged to a Highlander, George Macintosh, and David Dale, who in 1783 with Richard Arkwright and Robert Owen had founded the cotton mills at Lanark. Prior to investing in Turkey Red, Macintosh had manufactured cudbear, a vegetable dye taken from a species of lichen that grows on sea rocks. The colour obtained (purple) could be used only on wool or silk but it was also used to give depth and lustre to indigo blue. An indication of the fierce competition that must have existed in the textile manufacturing industry of the time is evident in the steps taken by Macintosh to protect his cudbear investment. He built a wall, ten feet high, around the cudbear works and then erected an elegant house within the walls, which he called Dunchattan ('Macintosh's stronghold'). He also swore his employees – a hand-picked group of Highlanders – to secrecy. One, however, eventually defected to London, taking the secret with him, and a cudbear works was set up in Westminster in 1793.

Macintosh and Dale also found it difficult to keep the secret of Turkey Red, a process which initially required about fifteen different steps and used such ingredients as sheep's dung, pearl ash, oil of vitriol and gum arabic. Macintosh and Dale had brought Pierre Jacques Papillon from Rouen to help start the dye works at Barrowfield. Papillon had the expertise needed to produce Turkey Red, but he proved a difficult employee, and two years after his arrival Macintosh wrote in a letter to his son, Charles: 'Papillon has now left us entirely. We could not manage his unhappy temper. I have made a great improvement in his process. I dye in 20 days what he took 25 to do and the colour is better.'[5] A subsequent notice in the *Glasgow Mercury* on 20 June 1789 announced that Peter James Papillon (he had anglicized his name)

Takes this opportunity of informing the public that he has set up a dye-house and has now begun to dye COTTON-YARN in RED, commonly called Turkey Red, of a colour superior to any that has been dyed in this country before, except by himself.

The dye works set up by Papillon at Rutherglen also advertised dyeing in blue, 'at different prices', green at two shillings (10p) per pound and yellow at one shilling and sixpence (7½p). By autumn the same newspaper was carrying a notice that the works had shut down. Papillon himself eventually retired from his unsuccessful business efforts, entrusting his money to his two sons, who lost it, leaving him destitute.

The secret of Turkey Red dye, of course, was not secret in Britain for long. Two French brothers had divulged the formula to the Manchester Chamber of Commerce in 1785 (the same year in which Macintosh and Dale set up their Glasgow dye works) and received a £2,500 reward from Parliament. The Glasgow Chamber of Commerce subsequently secured the 'secret' from the government and made it available to members of the Chamber. Macintosh and Dale had also shown specimens of their work to a Parliamentary committee who awarded them a cash prize, which they never received.

The production of Turkey Red cloth, called 'Dale's Red' locally, became such a thriving industry in the west of Scotland that the Statistical Account of Scotland in 1794 indicated there were 1,500 looms in the Glasgow area alone, which concentrated on producing cloth using Turkey Red, and that the colour was so fast that 'when woven into brown cotton or linen yarn it resists and stands the whole process of bleaching and acquires more beauty and lustre'. Bleaching itself had also become a flourishing business in the west of Scotland: as early as 1728 Glasgow manufacturers were sending linen to be bleached on the banks of Loch Lomond and on the Leven.

Macintosh and Dale flourished in the Turkey Red business (and Macintosh's son went on to add further lustre to the family name with his invention of a flexible waterproof material for raincoats – a coat known to this day as a Macintosh). However, after almost twenty years, Macintosh senior and Dale sold the Barrowfield dye works to Henry Monteith of Carstairs, the man responsible for giving Glasgow's Turkey Red industry a world-wide reputation. Monteith, at the age of twenty-four, was a muslin manufacturer. At the age of thirty-seven he started a weaving factory at Bridgeton making bandana handkerchiefs, and later in the same year (1802) took over a factory at Blantyre operated by his brother and started Turkey Red dyeing. He used the Turkey Red dye for woven handkerchiefs and bandanas and calico printing, not only improving the process over the years but becoming a major exporter. Henry Monteith died in 1848, at the age of eighty-four, having made his fortune on Turkey Red, and having served in public life as Lord Provost of Glasgow and as a Member of Parliament. His firm continued until 1904, when it was liquidated.

Notes

1. Stuart Robinson, *A History of Printed Textiles*, London, 1969, p.14.

2. Angus McLean (ed.), *Local Industries of Glasgow and the West of Scotland*, Glasgow: British Association, 1901, p.136.

3. Margaret Bennett (School of Scottish Studies), *Studies of the Hebridean Scots in the Eastern Townships of Quebec*, Ottawa: National Museums of Canada, 1980, p.79.

4. Larch S. Garrad, 'Quilting and Patchwork in the Isle of Man', *Folk Life*, Vol.17, 1979.

5. George Stewart, *Curiosities of Glasgow Citizenship*, Glasgow: James Maclehose, 1881.

3

PIECING AND PATTERNS

I hold the quilt in my hands.
The blue and white squares fall
Over my feet and out and over the floor.
The blue is twilight now and the white is white no more.[1]

Squares, it is said, are the oldest patchwork pattern – especially squares of various colours arranged in alternation with white. One nineteenth-century writer likened this arrangement to an imitation of the draughts or chequers board which can be traced back to the wine shops of Pompeii and a board game played there in A.D.70.[2] Certainly the square as a piecing shape figured prominently in the memories of Siobhan Ni Luian, who wrote the stanzas above as an opening to her reminiscences about a day spent quilting with friends. Possibly the square had been imposed on her as an essential patchwork shape since childhood, for in Siobhan's part of Ireland, at the turn of the century, one titled lady used to visit the parish schools regularly, leaving bundles of materials for the children to cut into squares and sew into quilts.

Rectangles, squares and long bands or strips are all shapes that are easily sewn together by beginning patchworkers or by needleworkers intent on making a quick utility quilt. In England, however, if one is to rely on existing evidence, squares never achieved the popularity of the hexagon.

HEXAGONS

Detail of Anna Brereton's patchwork.

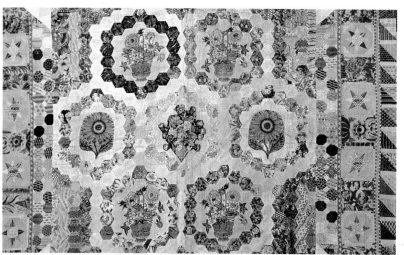

Called by a variety of names including honeycomb and sexagon (also 'optigons', 'octicians', 'sextains' and 'sixes' according to Elizabeth Hake),[3] the hexagon and variations on it, are known to have been used in England from the eighteenth century and probably earlier. An elongated version of the shape – called the Church Window by Averil Colby[4] or Lozenge or Pointed Oblong – appears in the Indian chintz quilt (circa 1708) at Levens Hall in Westmorland, along with the shapes of the cross and the octagon. Another version of the hexagon, called the coffin patch because the elongated hexagon shape has been squared off on two opposite ends, figures rather poignantly in the Brereton Hangings in the collection of Strangers' Hall in Norwich.

Anna Brereton made this patchwork coverlet in the early
nineteenth century while recovering from the loss of a child.
It features a medallion centre of six hexagon pieced rondels
with centres of Broderie Perse. The quilt has neither filling
nor quilting but is backed with white linen. 8 ft 11 in square
(272 cm). (Strangers' Hall, Norfolk Museums Service)

The Brereton Hangings, which are extensive and include not only valances and bed-curtains but also a patchwork quilt, all made in chintzes, are the work of Anna Margaretta Lloyd of Cardiganshire, Wales. In 1782 Anna married her cousin John Brereton and went to live in Brinton Hall, Norfolk. The couple's first son died in infancy and the second son at the age of fourteen, following an attack of fever. Distraught with grief, Anna refused to be comforted and almost a year elapsed before she was discovered designing patterns and putting pieces of chintz together. This sign of returning health was encouraged by those around her and the furnishings for the bed were begun. All of them were completed between 1801 and 1805, by which time Anna was completely restored to health. The coffin patch was used frequently in the pieced work of the bed-hangings which she made, as well as appliqué. Her quilt, however, contained hexagons – six hexagon rondels are featured in the medallion centre (see page 52). Anna's daughter also proved a keen needlewoman: the collection in Norwich, which is actually housed in Strangers' Hall, also contains window curtains and chair-covers made by her. Strangers' Hall, an old mansion which is now a museum of domestic life, obtained its name in the sixteenth century with the arrival of many settlers from Europe, notably The Netherlands. These Dutch immigrants did much to help develop the textile industry in the area.

Most of the hexagon quilts that have survived date from the 1800s, and invariably they show a preference for using the hexagon shape in Grandmother's Flower Garden (sometimes in Wales called Flower in the Field). This is the pattern in which rosettes composed of seven hexagon pieces are linked by a common light or dark hexagon piece, thus giving the effect of a scattered collection of flowers. Many of the old hexagon quilts, however, were assembled with little regard to the placing of the pieces or the overall design, unlike the six-sided table cover on page 55 made by Mrs Anne Loney, a gardener's wife who lived in Perthshire in Scotland. Mrs Loney's cover was made about 1840 (it is believed she obtained scraps for her sewing from Fingask Castle, Raith, the home of her husband's employers) and she didn't stop at the table cover, for she also made a matching tea cosy and a quilt, the latter now in the collection of Perth Museum. Several of these six-sided table covers exist in British collections. One of the earliest dates from 1780 and is made of cotton – it is in the collection of the Welsh Folk Museum at St Fagans. Most of the six-sided covers, however, have been made in satin, silk and velvet hexagons. One

unfinished six-sided cover in the collection of the Dundee Museums and Art Galleries, however, has been pieced with diamonds which radiate from a central star. Fragments of the newspaper, the *Dundee Courier,* dated 1880 have been basted on the surface of the cloth, presumably to protect the fabrics from marking during sewing.

The hexagon has continued to be a popular shape to the present day in Britain, and many beginning patchworkers almost regard it as essential to their piecing initiation. The basic challenge with this shape remains – it still takes an observant and creative needlewoman to choose fabrics and place templates in such a way that the printed pattern is used to best advantage. The late Averil Colby, who wrote extensively about patchwork and quilting, was also a skilled needlewoman and one who was particularly fond of the hexagon shape. One of the most challenging quilts she ever assembled is pictured in her book, *Patchwork.* The quilt features a hexagon wreath as a central medallion. Each hexagon shape in the wreath is a flower or leaf cut from an assortment of printed cottons and sewn together in such a way that from a distance it resembles a whole.

The popularity of Turkey Red twill in the mid-nineteenth century also influenced the hexagon shape, in that the colour became popular for linking and outlining hexagon piecing. Dorinda suggested Turkey Red twill to connect hexagon 'stars' (another name for rosettes) but only if using cotton. If using silk, she advised, one had to link the stars with black.[5] The quilt on page 56 is a good example of how Turkey Red twill was used as an emphasis. An unfinished quilt in the collection of Liverpool Museums shows a variation: instead of rosettes or stars, hexagons have been sewn in alternating clusters of three identical prints and three Turkey Red pieces. Another recommended combination was sewing together strips of either diamonds or hexagons, alternating red and white pieces in one row and then adding two rows of plain white pieces, so as to space out the colour. Sometimes the black hexagon suggested by Dorinda, however, proved more appealing: one 'couvre-pied' (sofa rug) written about in glowing terms consisted of black satin hexagons with the occasional inset of a piece of rich brocade in brilliant colours, and it was compared to the effect of 'glowing jewels' in a dark setting and was judged an 'artist's inspiration' – it was lined with brightly-coloured satin and trimmed with gold silk cord.[6]

The advent of Turkey Red twill seemed to inspire a number of design ideas. The appearance of a red cloth that did not run or shrink appealed not only to

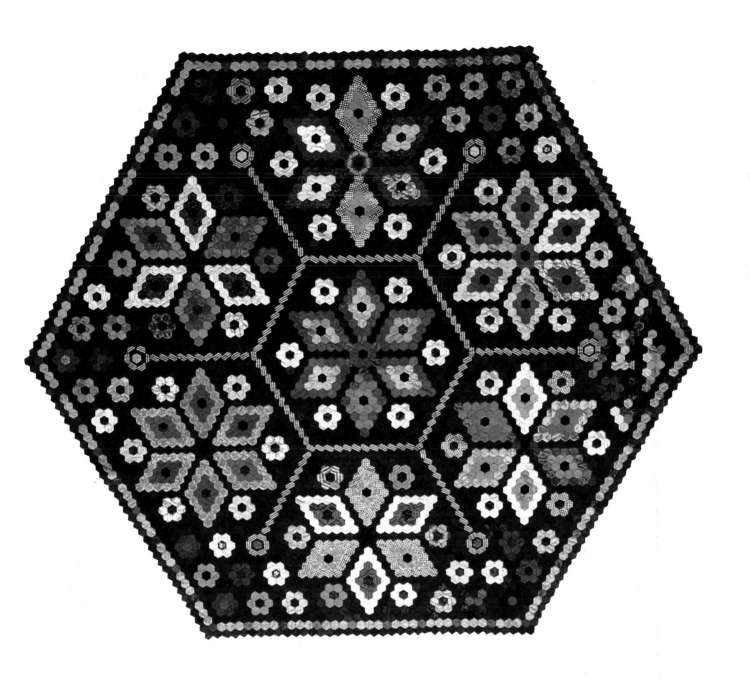

Six-sided hexagon table cloth made of silk, velvet, brocade, ribbon and taffeta scraps by Mrs Anne Loney about 1840. Mrs Loney's husband was a gardener at Fingask Castle, Raith, Perthshire, and the scraps of material she used came from the castle household. Diameter 6 ft 4 in (193 cm). (City of Dundee Museums and Art Galleries)

English hexagon quilt featuring Turkey Red twill outlining and border of triangles pieced into squares. Backed but unquilted and sewn by hand with papers that are still intact. Made in 1870. 6 ft × 8 ft (183 cm × 244 cm). (Strangers' Hall, Norfolk Museums Service)

Pieced Turkey Red lily blocks with appliquéd stems. Made in
Ireland about 1880 and quilted with waves. 6 ft 5 in square
(196 cm). (Ulster Folk and Transport Museum)

Basket quilt pieced in pink and green and white cotton. The baskets are hand-pieced with machine appliquéd handles and the quilting is done in diagonal lines. Made in Llandysul, Dyfed, about 1870. 5 ft 3 in × 6 ft 2 in (160 cm × 188 cm).
(Jen Jones)

Green, cream and yellow cotton sateen quilt made by Mrs
Matilda Clish of Annfield Plain, County Durham, about 1907.
The quilting follows the piecing pattern. Mrs Clish made two
of these quilts – one for each of her daughters. 6 ft × 7 ft 3 in
(183 cm × 221 cm). (Beamish North of England Open Air
Museum)

Above: Pink and blue cotton pieced quilt with alternating blocks of white print squares. Quilted with circle and leaf pattern and edged with blue border. Made near Merthyr Tydfil in 1860. 7 ft 1 in × 7 ft 8 in (216 cm × 234 cm). (Jen Jones)

Right: Striped cot quilt made by Mrs Arabella Thompson of Belfast prior to 1890. The quilt is made of blocks of overlapping folded strips of scrap fabrics which have been sewn to a ground. Red cotton sateen is used for both the frill and the backing. 3 ft 5 in × 4 ft 8 in (104 cm × 142 cm). (Ulster Folk and Transport Museum)

quiltmakers but to women looking for a heavy twill that could be used in rough domestic furnishings or work clothing. It was cheerful and it brought warmth to dull interiors. Red flannel had been used previously in utility quilts but it was not satisfactory because the colour was not fast. It would certainly not withstand the annual spring wash ritual in Ireland when quilts were put in a tub of Rinso and soft soap:

'. . . we used to get in and dance on the winter quilts and this helped to take some of the dirt out of them. We did think it very exciting . . . we had great fun . . . you could step in the tub and dance around this helped to take the first of the dirt out.'[7]

Squares of Turkey Red, alternated with white, became an almost compulsory combination in Bazaar and Bible quilts (see Chapter 5) where embroidery played a significant role. It was declared by one needlework writer in 1888 that Turkey Red actually looked better with a little embroidery:

This upon the Turkey twill looks best done in cross-stitch with white ingrain cotton, and can easily be managed by laying a piece of Berlin wool canvas over the square, working the cross-stitch through this and the twill, and when it is finished drawing away the threads of canvas one by one.[8]

Turkey Red was also used extensively in appliqué techniques. There almost seemed to be a compulsion to match the red with white – perhaps the novelty of being able to link two such disparate colours, without fear of bleeding, was in itself the motive. The Irish in particular were fond of the red and white combinations, and surviving quilts show that it was used in variations of the Log Cabin pattern and in the pattern commonly called Peter and Paul – which in Ireland was termed Churn Dash. (The pattern was also called 'Jockey Cap'. A fine pink and white quilt in this design, circa 1900, is in the collection of the Bowes Museum at Barnard Castle, County Durham.) The Turkey Red quilt also appears in the collection in the Manx Museum in the Isle of Man, where it has been used in Log Cabin patterns and hexagon appliqué or in blocks of squares, rectangles and triangles in a pattern which in Canada is called Chimney Sweep and in the United States Courthouse Square.

SEWING TECHNIQUES

The piecing of hexagons, or for that matter diamonds or triangles, was invariably done with paper templates made of old letters, pages from exercise books or pieces of card, the pieces of cotton first being basted on the paper, and then the edges oversewn. This technique is still used today under the title of the 'English Method' of piecing, to distinguish it from the American preference for piecing with running stitches and without paper templates, although the running stitch was also used in Britain for sewing patchwork – especially when large geometrical pieces were put together. Sewing with papers may take longer and suggest being a bit on the 'fussy' side, but it has always offered greater precision in piecing, a fact which became apparent with the more complicated piecing patterns undertaken by the Victorians, where individual patches could be less than one inch.

Quilts that still have their papers intact are a godsend to historians, since they often help with dating the work. Even the basting stitches which still hold the papers in place are helpful clues – if only for separating the truly proficient needlewomen from the beginners. Mrs Loney, the creator of the six-sided hexagon cloth described earlier, was in the former category. She did not use papers for sewing, but rather hexagon shapes cut from a type of buckram, the fabric normally used for stiffening. Nor did she follow the usual practice of basting each piece from the back to the front which would require removal of all basting threads at conclusion. Mrs Loney carefully folded each point of the hexagon over the one-inch buckram template and then took only six basting stitches at the back – each stitch placed at a strategic fold. With her method it was unnecessary to remove either template or basting.

The method of sewing with papers did, of course, require two template patterns – one for cutting the fabric and the second for cutting the slightly smaller paper around which the fabric was basted. These templates, usually made in zinc or tin, were cut to order by the local tinsmith or ironmonger. Once all the pieces had been basted on paper and sewn together – very accurately, from point to point – the papers were removed and the completed patchwork, except in the case of velvet, was ironed from the back before a lining was attached.

Patchworkers were advised to be methodical in approach: *How to Make Common Things,* a book written for girls in 1890, recommended that the only way in which to commence making patchwork was first to make a bag in which to collect scraps from 'all quarters because in order to make pretty and effective work, we must have plenty of choice in colours and patterns'.[9] The scraps were to be sorted into dark, light and 'half-tints' and the patches made up in the same order, each being tacked neatly with a fine needle and cotton on its paper template and then oversewn with fine cotton or fine silk depending on the type of fabric being used. 'The utmost perfection of stitching is needed, or the work will be spoilt, as each stitch shows.'[10]

A further indication of the sewing habits of the nineteenth-century patchworker and the contents of her sewing-box can be gleaned from the items in a twentieth-century auction. The items in this instance belonged to a middle-class woman, a Miss B— (1819–99) from Essex, whose belongings were described as 'The Property of a Lady' and sold in three lots. Among the items offered:

A collection of needlework accessories including an egg-shaped basket with bracelet handle trimmed with ivory silk ribbon; two straw-work boxes . . . printed paper box containing six reels of white cotton with painted wooden tops resembling flowers . . . a Queen Victoria's Jubilee Commemorative medallion . . . A collection of paper and metal templates for patchwork and a quantity of silk, velvet and cotton patchwork pieces and scraps – in printed paper and wooden boxes including a Havana cigar box . . . some of the templates contained in Fred K. Joyce's Percussion Gun Powder and Caps jars – all in a domed trunk by J. Emes 123 New Bond Street London . . . A collection of unfinished patchwork pieces including Baby Block and Grandmother's Flower Garden; two patchwork bags and two pillowcases, a piece of silk patchwork and two lengths of printed cotton.[11]

LOG CABIN

The pieced block commonly referred to as 'Log Cabin' appears often in collections of patchwork in Ireland and Scotland and its origins are commonly attributed to North America. Indeed, if one accepts the explanation for the traditional colour mix of the block – a red centre surrounded by two sides of light strips and two sides of dark strips – then the symbolism of the design seems all the more appropriate. It is commonly supposed that the colour red in this popular bit of piecing denotes the fireplace, and the dark and light shades the shadows and light thrown by the fire on the log walls. Tracing this pattern back, however, not only reveals name changes (a common enough problem in tracing patchwork patterns) but possibly a different design source.

One book published for young girls just before the end of the nineteenth century first termed this pattern 'Canadian Logwood' but then stated that it should more appropriately be termed

Egyptian or Mummy pattern, as numerous bands of linen arranged in this manner have been found covering the swathing bands of mummies, two or three thousand years old. These may be seen in the British, Oxford, and other museums. The patchwork is arranged with perfect symmetry and forms a highly decorative wrapper.[12]

Perhaps the author of this particular chapter on patchwork was something of an Egyptologist in the first place.

Ten years before this, the *Dictionary of Needlework* by S.F.A. Caulfield had also attributed the pattern to Canada and called it 'Loghouse Quilting', although in this instance there was no quilting, and the 'logs' were made of ribbon and sewn to a backing in such a way that they overlapped each other instead of being stitched edge to edge. An example of this overlapping technique can be seen in both the Log Cabin quilt on page 66 and the Irish cot quilt on page 61, although in the latter instance the loghouse or cabin blocks were not used – only the overlapping technique.

The Log Cabin block was also called 'straight patchwork' and described as an 'old pattern of the West Country' in M.K. Gifford's *Needlework*, believed to have been published at the turn of this century in London, and the 'roof pattern' in the Isle of Man in the nineteenth century – but largely because of the manner in which the blocks were assembled, colours being arranged to provide a strong diagonal zig-zag. In fact, Log Cabin was described as the 'true Manx pattern' of the Isle of Man, the other two basic types of patchwork practised being 'pieced patchwork', with paper templates and oversewing, and the 'typical Manx style of pieced patchwork – in which large squares, rectangles and bands' were joined with a running stitch.[13]

Extant British quilts which feature the Log Cabin pattern date back to the first half of the nineteenth century and they are made of every type of fabric, including wool. The pineapple Log Cabin from Larne (illustrated on page 64) featured red flannel centres and a mixture of cotton and wool. There was also a vogue for using the Log Cabin pattern in only two colours – Turkey Red and white. This was done in Ireland, Scotland and the Isle of Man – sometimes the blocks were assembled in a

Pineapple Log Cabin quilt made from a mixture of red
flannel, cotton and wool, and backed with a black print.
Made in Larne about 1840. 6 ft × 6 ft 11 in (183 cm ×
211 cm). (Ulster Folk and Transport Museum)

Two sisters who were dressmakers in Kellyleagh, County
Down, sewed this unusual Log Cabin variation in 1880. The
quilt is made from yellow, brown and grey cotton. 5 ft 9 in ×
5 ft 11 in (176 cm × 180 cm). (Ulster Folk and Transport
Museum)

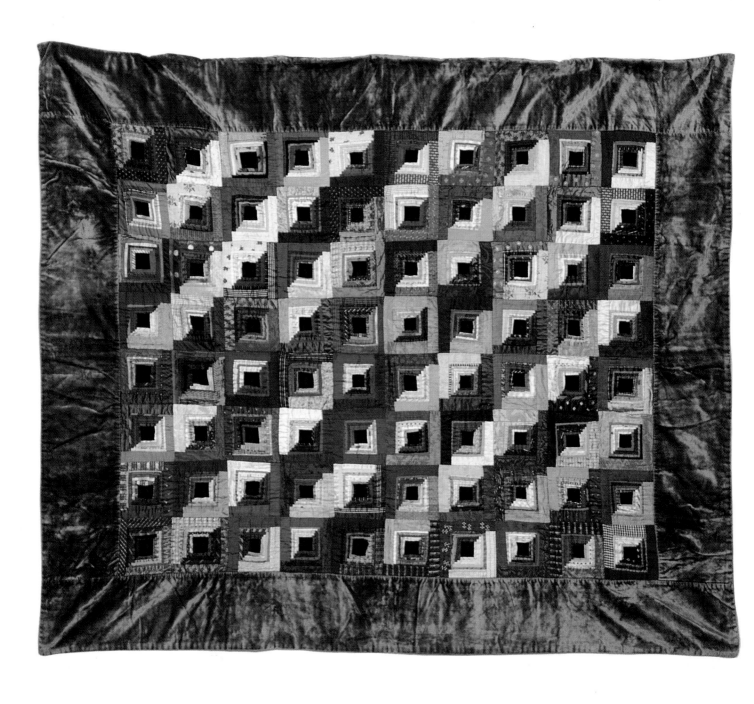

Log Cabin quilt of silks and satins with a gold plush velvet
border and sateen back. The 'logs' have been sewn to a
ground in doubled overlapping strips. It has a blanket filling
and rough hand-quilted four-leaf clovers. 5 ft × 6 ft 1 in
(152 cm × 185 cm). (Ann Carswell)

Log Cabin table cover made of silks and satins and a plush
velvet border edged with tatted lace. Made in England about
1890. 4 ft 1 in square (124 cm). (The Castle Museum, York)

Each of the Log Cabin centres of this table cover has been hand-embroidered with a different flower.

cruciform, with four white sides forming the cross. Two very fine matching quilts of this description are in the collection of the Ceres Folk Museum in Fife. The white crosses stand out on the red ground and the scalloped borders have been embroidered with white leaves and flowers.

The Victorians, of course, used silks, velvets, brocades, satins and ribbons in their Log Cabin work. Some of these fabrics were so heavy that the only way to sew them was to follow the practice of overlapping and stitch one side only to a backing cloth or ground. The Log Cabin pattern was in many ways the perfect vehicle for the fancy work embraced by the Victorians. The centre of the block was an ideal ground for embroidery. The table cover on page 67 is a good example – each block has a hand-embroidered centre.

Although extant British Log Cabin quilts go back only to the early nineteenth century, there is good reason to believe that the origin of this design is much older and that it was probably carried to North America by emigrants. Averil Colby wrote of a Stirlingshire woman who possessed Log Cabin quilts made from patterns handed down in the family since the 'Forty-Five'.[14] (The Jacobite Rising of 1745, when Prince Charles Edward Stuart –

'Bonnie Prince Charlie' – made an ill-fated attempt to gain the British throne by force of arms.) Some of these quilts, according to Mrs Colby, were made 'wholly of tweed and homespun woollen stuff'. The pattern appears even earlier, however, on a square English perfume bag worked in latticed silks and dated 1650.[15] In this instance the blocks have been assembled in a cruciform shape, with the dark sides turned to the centre.

One interesting theory about the origin of the Log Cabin pattern lies neither in thriftiness (the pattern does require a number of small scraps) nor in the symbolism of domestic hearths and man-made walls. Rather it has to do with the land itself and the way in which it was cultivated until the late 1600s.[16]

Communal tenancy farming was once widespread in Scotland, Ireland and in parts of continental Europe also. In Scotland, in fact, until the late 1600s, there were more communal tenancy farms than single tenancy farms. The fields worked in these farms were arranged in strips called 'run-rigs' (strip farming had also been practised earlier in Britain during the Roman occupation). The run-rig system of cultivation allowed for both 'infields' and 'outfields'. The former were not only more arable and wetter, they were also treated with all available manure and were constantly seeded with grain crops. The 'outfields', on the other hand, were drier, stonier and less productive.[17] Because of the primitive conditions of farming – implements were basic and improved drainage unknown – it was arranged that everyone was allocated an equal portion of wet and dry fields, so that each could harvest at least one crop.

An examination of early maps – especially those which show strip or run-rig farming in both Scotland and Roman England – make the pattern connection much easier.[18] The fields are laid out in blocks of parallel strips which run at right angles to each other. It needs only a small leap of the imagination to conclude that the colour red, which has always been the traditional centre of the Log Cabin block, represents not fire but the sun, and that the light and dark sides of the block represent the wet and dry strip fields.

THE VICTORIANS

The real patchwork challenge in so far as piecing was concerned developed with the Victorians and their obsession with 'Fancy Work'. Sewing squares, rectangles or even hexagons was easy compared with the intricate patterns that women were being encouraged to sew by the periodicals of the late

nineteenth century. Patchwork changed its status with the Victorians – it moved from the bedroom to the parlour, and instead of quilts being considered as purely utilitarian objects they became ornamental. Women were encouraged to piece ottoman covers, fringed pillows, antimacassars, even window blinds. The penchant for luxury fabrics like silk, satin and velvet made the actual sewing more difficult; compared with cotton, these materials offered special problems in assembly – and cotton had become vulgar!

Patchwork, during the Victorian era, vied with a large number of other needlework pursuits like Berlin wool work and lace-making. *Sylvia's Home Journal,* a lively mix of fiction, fashion, book reviews and interviews, is one of many that carried a monthly needlework feature. Most of the patterns on offer were for knitting, crochet, embroidery and macramé. Indeed, but for the fact that the magazine had monthly advertisements like 'Patchwork 200 pieces of silks, satins, and brocades, pattern and a diagram for 1s 4d. M.L. care of Sylvia' or 'Patchwork six dozen pieces of silks, satins and brocades, all new 1s 6d' also care of Sylvia, one might wonder if the editors of the magazine were less than sympathetic towards this particular type of needle art. In fact there was a delightful put-down for one concerned reader in 1884:

Mabel writes: Dear Sylvia, Could any of your readers tell me the way to work silk patchwork for sofa cushions etc. I have no idea whatever of the cutting out, arranging, or putting together; also how to make it into what is called mosaic work by working stars and other things on it with crewel silk. Full particulars would greatly oblige.

The editor's reply was less than helpful:

There are various kinds of patchwork. You will find it difficult to learn how to do the work from instructions only. If you write again, will you kindly use only one side of each sheet of paper.

Perhaps Sylvia felt some remorse, for in September that year, in an article on 'Novelties in Needlework', which suggested making firescreens out of peacock's plumes and winter bonnets and carriage rugs from feathers, she had this to say:

Patchwork is now so elaborate that it does not in the least resemble the work that used formerly to be used under that name. One of the latest ideas is to make the work of diamonds of coloured silk or satin arranged, of course, with a due regard to the blending of the colours. A fine gold cord or braid is tacked along rather tightly all the seams where the diamonds are joined so that it has the effect of parti-coloured quilting. Sometimes the feather stitch is substituted for the cord.

In addition to a monthly classified ad column, *Sylvia's Home Journal* also featured a 'Free Exchange Column'. Some interesting nuggets of information can be gleaned from these: in 1885, for example, a Miss Grey from Kent was looking for offers to exchange an embroidered quilt of pink

sateen and velvet with cream insertion and lace 'valued at 2 guineas'; and in 1888 a Miss Skelton from York indicated that she was willing to exchange a 'lovely crazy patchwork bracket drapery, worked in silk, satin, plush and velvet, ornamented with tinsel and spangles' for a 'good clean well-bound book suitable for gumming pictures in or lady's work basket lined with satin, which must be in good condition, or small box Rowney's moist water colours'.

The advertisements in the magazine also give an idea of patterns and fabrics. In 1883, ninepence (3½p) would have bought the instructions for making an 'elegant counterpane' of Turkey Red twill and scraps of white calico; in 1894 the diagrams for cutting papers for 'The Twist, Oriel and Mexican Stripe' were on offer for thirteen stamps; in 1888 it was possible to buy a gross of stars

Above: Section of velvet star quilt made about 1875 by a Miss Miller, a seamstress who made shirts for King George V. 5 ft 10 in × 6 ft 4 in (178 cm × 193 cm). (Ulster Folk and Transport Museum)

Below: Detail of star block used in woollen patchwork quilt. Made in the late nineteenth century. 6 ft 8 in × 6 ft 10 in (203 cm × 208 cm). (Ulster Folk and Transport Museum)

Early Victorian ribbon quilt made from bonnet ties and backed with blue wool. The quilt has been machine-quilted in diamonds. 5 ft 6 in × 5 ft 10 in (168 cm × 180 cm). (Ulster Folk and Transport Museum)

Velvet sampler quilt. Patterns include hexagons, Log Cabin, crazy patchwork and baby blocks. The quilt has a blanket filling and a print backing and is unquilted. Made in England in the late nineteenth century. 5 ft 4 in × 5 ft 5 in (163 cm × 165 cm). (Ann Carswell)

Table cover with central medallion star, pieced chiefly with wool scraps and edged with a braid border. Backed but unquilted. Made in England about 1900. 3 ft 4 in square (102 cm). (The Castle Museum, York)

Victorian table cover sewn with overlapping gathered clam shells in satin, taffeta, ribbon and velvet. The green wool edge is crocheted, and the velvet centre and four extending strips are decorated with lines from hymns reproduced in crystal bead work. 'Lonely? No Not Lonely while Jesus Standeth By' is the opening line in the hymn reproduced in the centre. The hymn quoted in the side panels, 'Thy Way not Mine O Lord', is by Horatius Bonar. Made in England in the late nineteenth century. 3 ft 9 in square (114 cm). (The Castle Museum, York)

Above: Silk patchwork cot cover made in 1870. 2 ft 2 in × 3 ft 2 in (66 cm × 97 cm). (Photograph courtesy of the Welsh Folk Museum)

Right: Victorian scrap quilt with velvet horseshoe, embroidered sunflower and printed ribbon, 'Carr Lane School Committee' made about 1890. No wadding or quilting. Backed with fine cotton. 5 ft 2 in × 6 ft 7 in (157 cm × 201 cm). (Ann Carswell)

and spangles for crazy patchwork for a shilling (5p); and in 1891, ninepence would have bought seventy new pieces of ribbon for patchwork. Perhaps it was just such an advertisement for ribbon that inspired quilts like the one on page 70.

The extent to which mosaic tile and parquetry designs were adapted for Victorian patchwork can be seen simply by comparing existing Victorian architecture with late nineteenth-century patchwork patterns and by the names of some patterns. Victorian tenements and houses alike invariably featured at least one tiled floor or wall – if only in the entry. In fact, the term mosaic patchwork developed from this association, although the term was broadened to include inlay work, which is described in Chapter 4, and the piecing of geometric patterns generally.

The relationship between the piecing of cloth and

the piecing of floors can be seen not only in the names of the patterns but in their composition. The 'Dutch Tile' pattern, the simplest mosaic to execute, was composed only of octagons and squares. Another, slightly more complicated pattern, had Lozenges – it is shown in Figure 1. Figure 2 was actually called 'Pavement Patchwork', while Figure 3 was called 'Minton'.

Not everyone was capable of achieving the intricate patterns on offer – one drawing adapted from the Weldon's Needlework series of the 1880s (Figure 4) shows a pattern intended to be worked as either a quilt centre or cushion cover in silks, satins and velvet. It is not for the inexperienced needlewoman. The completed work was meant to

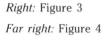

be only eighteen inches across, and although ribbon was recommended – mitred at the corners – for the several border edges, the real challenge lay in adopting the right colours and in the precise stitching of the many different shapes required to make up the pattern.

Perhaps mosaic work was popular for the challenge it offered in stitching. Or perhaps it simply fitted with the fussiness of the period. May Morris compared it to the colour and design of mosaic tile work in the East:

It is rather difficult to give a clear idea of this curious embroidery by mere description. You must imagine a mosaic as it were, but instead of being made up of bits of marble or coloured glass, this mosaic is formed of pieces of stuff of different colours, fitted together in certain ornamental shapes and finished with touches of colour in embroidery stitches. Such patchwork distinctly comes into the category of things artistic, while the quilts and such like of the last and present centuries are only pretty pieces of neat stitchery in which an elementary sense of geometric design and colour yet remains in the sometime clever arrangement of the different scraps of dress stuff of which they are composed.[19]

Baby blocks (also called the 'box pattern') were a popular patchwork pattern during this era, as well as hexagons, Log Cabin and, of course, crazy patchwork. One quilt which managed to demonstrate all of these favourites is that shown on page 71. Stars made up of six diamonds, surrounded by a dark outlining colour, or diamond stars worked with squares, were other favourites. Sections from two quilts on page 69 demonstrate this. One quilt was made entirely of velvets and the other is a mix of Turkey Red twill and wool.

The Lozenge, a pointed oblong or elongated hexagon, continued to be a shape which found favour with the Victorians. It appeared in a number of the floor tile-like patterns and in the lattice pattern: four lozenges of the same colour are sewn to form a star and black velvet squares are used as infill. A table cover in the collection of the Ceres Folk Museum in Fife features this pattern. The edges of the cover have not been squared off but left as points; and the piece, made about 1883, has been backed with a cut-down Paisley shawl.

The Lozenge appeared, too, in a complex mosaic pattern worked with squares in *The Dictionary of Needlework* by Caulfield (see Figure 5). The directions for this particular mosaic clearly illustrate not only the colour preferences of the Victorians but the fact that sewing instructions of the time were not always easy to follow. The recommended colours for this particular pattern were black and yellow satin, and red and purple silk. Another pattern by Caulfield called 'Jewel' (see

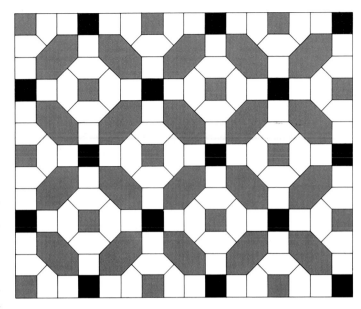

Figure 6) was intended to be made in such a way that each square represented light falling on a cut stone. In order to achieve this effect, it was suggested that blocks be composed of two different shades of blue satin brocade and ruby, emerald and yellow brocade. The connecting strips were to be 'plain brown gold satin'.

The Victorians employed various geometric shapes to embellish the hexagon. The 'Double Twisted Hexagon' shown in Figure 7 was a variation on the 'Twist', a pattern which featured octagons and squares and a narrow bar, with one end squared off and the other sloped to a point. The arrangement of the pieces is such that the bar interlaces itself around the octagons and squares.

Some Victorian patchwork shapes seem never to have survived much beyond the turn of the century. 'Scale armour', a pattern shown in Figure 8, is one of

Figure 5

Figure 6

Figure 7

Figure 8

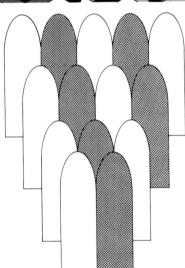

The patchwork technique also extended to other forms of domestic use. Kid was used for small items like slippers or mats, cut in simple geometric patterns, oversewn from the back and then couched from the front with cord or braid to cover the seam. Morocco leather was also considered a suitable fabric for patchwork for note cases, mats and book bindings, although it was usually glued on a backing instead of sewn. And patchwork was used for carriage rugs. Squares were cut out of suitings and worsted wools called 'cloth', then bound with decorative braid or ribbon and sewn together.

Indeed, as far as patchwork history is concerned, the challenge taken up by the Victorians is one of the most absorbing. The designs may have been fussy, the colours vulgar, the fabrics too elaborate and the finished work impractical, but no one can deny the technical achievement of the needlewomen of the time.

Notes

1. Rose Emerson, 'Quilting', *Journal of The Glens of Antrim Historical Society,* Vol. 4, 1976.

2. Dora de Blaquiere, et al., *How to Make Common Things: A Handy Book for Girls,* London, 1890.

3. Elizabeth Hake, *English Quilting Old and New,* London, 1937.

4. Averil Colby, *Patchwork,* London, 1958.

5. Dorinda, *Needlework for Ladies for Pleasure and Profit,* London, 1883.

6. M.K. Gifford, *Needlework* (The Hobby Books), London, n.d., p.147.

7. Oral history recording by Linda Ballard, Ulster Folk and Transport Museum.

8. B.C. Saward, 'Needlework Suggestions', *The Housewife,* Vol. 3, London, 1888, p.209.

9. de Blaquiere, op. cit., p.39.

10. Ibid., p.40.

11. Christie's, South Kensington. Textile sale catalogue for 16 December 1986.

12. Mary Whitley (ed.), *Every Girl's Book of Sport, Occupation and Pastime,* London, 1897, p.102.

13. Larch S. Garrad, 'Quilting and Patchwork in the Isle of Man', *Folk Life,* Vol. 17, 1979, p.42.

14. Colby, op. cit., p.66.

15. G. Saville Seligman and E. Talbot Hughes, *Domestic Needlework,* London: Country Life, 1926, Plate 58.

16. I am indebted to Robert Smith, Curator of the Auchindrain Museum of Country Life, near Inveraray, for first suggesting the correlation.

17. A more detailed explanation can be found in I.F. Grant, *Highland Folk Ways,* London, 1961, Ch. 5.

18. Ibid., p.45 (diagram of a Highland settlement). Illustrations of the strip farming practised by the Romans can be seen in H.P.R. Finberg (ed.), *The Agrarian History of England and Wales,* Cambridge, 1972, Vol. I, A.D. 43–1042, p.92.

19. May Morris, *Decorative Needlework,* London, 1893, Ch. 5.

these. Another was the quill pattern, also featured in Weldon's series, in which scraps of silk were folded to form pointed quills and then sewn in overlapping rows on a firm backing. One of the most unusual shapes, however, was the gathered overlapping clam shell. It is the main patchwork pattern in the unusual Hymn or Bible table cover on page 73 and it is worked in silk, satin and ribbon and taffeta, with the lettering done in crystal beads. The pattern appeared in the third series of *Weldon's Practical Patchwork,* published in the late nineteenth century, and it was initially recommended as a decorative outline or border around a lattice-worked glove sachet. In the case of the table cover mentioned, each clam shell is doubled, gathered and sewn to a backing.

4

APPLIQUÉ AND INLAY

The application of one fabric to another – appliqué – is an old embroidery technique which has been traced back to Siberia and the fourth century B.C.[1] It appears in the historic needlework collections of many countries – both European and Eastern – and in many diverse forms. Crude figures of Tristram and Iseult, roughly applied and outlined with cord, feature in a fifteenth-century German cloth-hanging in the collection of the Victoria and Albert Museum, London, while a nineteenth-century woman's jacket from Hungary, in the same collection, shows elaborate floral appliqué in leather.

Much of the applied work of the sixteenth and seventeenth centuries was ecclesiastical but some was also domestic. Mary Queen of Scots, a most prolific needlewoman, brought bed-hangings and canopies for twenty beds when she returned to Scotland from France in 1561, including at least one in 'appliqué of satin in four colours, red, blue, yellow and white, bordered with "false gold" and silver'.[2] And Mary continued to be involved in the refurbishment of more beds during her reign in Scotland, sometimes cutting up gold and silver vestments for appliqué work.

Indeed, the Elizabethan Age (1558–1603) was considered by many to be the second of two great eras in English embroidery, and the prodigious output of domestic needlework included bed-curtains, valances and coverlets decorated with embroidery and appliqué.

In so far as the appliqué technique was used in the making of quilts or coverlets in Britain, several distinct fashions stand out, the first starting with a craze for Indian chintzes.

——BRODERIE PERSE/CRETONNE APPLIQUÉ——

The technique of cutting printed flowers and trees from one length of fabric and applying them to another, called Broderie Perse or Cretonne Appliqué, can be linked to the demand for Indian chintzes that began in the seventeenth century. Both the glazed Indian chintzes and cretonne chintz, an unglazed print which originated in France, were widely used for appliquéd covers.

Between 1600 and 1800, when India was the world's greatest exporter of textiles, chintz was highly prized in Europe and also, at one point, very scarce: in 1701 the brightly-coloured imported prints had become so popular that they were barred from Britain because of the economic threat they posed to the country's own textile industry.

Chintz had been arriving in London in small quantities since the early 1600s, following the founding of the East India Company. The appeal of Indian chintz lay not only in its brilliant colourings but in the fact that the dyes used by Indian craftsmen contained mordant, a fixing agent. The Indian dyes were then in advance of those being employed in Europe. The first prints to arrive were coarse, block-printed and primitive in design; the finer chintzes which followed were painted.

In 1643 a director of the East India Company wrote to the company agent in Surat, requesting a change in background colour from red to white. This is the earliest recorded attempt to change the indigenous Indian design, and it followed a disappointing London auction of 'Pintadoe Quilts' by the Company.[3] ('Pintadoe' was the Portuguese word for cotton painting.) That modification proved highly successful for the Company and further

Scrap quilt which includes Toile de Jouy prints from France. Made in 1800. 9 ft square (274 cm). (Strangers' Hall, Norfolk Museums Service)

Centre of the Dacre quilt showing pheasant, palm tree and circlet of flowers.

westernization of Indian patterns followed. The popular design of a flowering tree, for example, which had arrived in India from Persia in the fifteenth century, had consisted originally of a serpentine trunk growing on a rockery, the branches sprouting a mixture of fruits and flowers. By the beginning of the eighteenth century, in deference to the market in the West, the tree had acquired such flowers as tulips, roses and chrysanthemums.[4]

Chinoiserie, a term which describes the European adaptation of Chinese motifs in ornament and design, was also fashionable in the seventeenth century. It, too, became part of chintz design because of a combination of influences: Indian chintzes were actually printed with chinoiserie ornament for the English market and also used in

applied work. Chinoiserie was also used in embroidery: one quilt worked in 1694 by Sarah Thurston of Challok in Kent appeared in an exhibition in Scotland in 1934. Brightly-coloured Chinese silks had been embroidered on a white satin ground in a manner 'at once restrained and spirited. The imagination displayed in the variety and group of pagodas, trees, flowers, birds and insects, is great. In the centre is the willow pattern in colours surrounded by an orle of flowers.'[5]

The growth of the printed textile industry in Britain – spurred on by the popularity of the Indian imports – is another factor of interest to quilt historians, especially in identifying certain prints. In 1719 there were thirty calico printers in London, and by 1851, the year of the Great Exhibition, over 200 in the UK as a whole. The output of these printers is worthy of many volumes but some trends help to place fabrics in context: it is known, for example, that London and Dublin textile printers were using copper-plate printing (the development of which undermined the Indian trade) to produce pastoral, theatrical, military, floral and figure designs in the late 1770s. The famous Toiles de Jouy, which also relied on copper-plate printing, and often used only one colour, were also being made in France at about the same time. The toiles from the Jouy workshop often had a historical theme – one print made about 1783 showed a romanticized picture of American Indians welcoming the nations of Europe; others were pastoral and one was extremely unusual in that it pictured the many different methods and stages used in the preparation and printing and finishing of the textiles at Jouy. At the beginning of the 1800s, the exotic designs based on Indian, Egyptian and Chinese themes, which were then so popular in Europe, gave way to a different trend, the new patterns depicting game birds, palm trees and classical architecture. In the 1830s there was even one Carlisle printer producing textiles which celebrated important new buildings like the Lime Street Station in Liverpool and Euston Station, London. These latter designs reflected the British public's enchantment with the new railways.

The textiles which had large figurative designs were particularly appropriate for Broderie Perse and the technique, when used, seemed to be confined to applying the cut-out prints. These were not only arranged in groupings, sometimes with a central medallion of a wreath of flowers, or of the flowering tree, which was also a favourite, but were often scattered on a white ground like a handful of seed. Putting a backing on the appliqué ground or quilting these Broderie Perse coverlets was

The work on this fine example of Broderie Perse was begun by Margaret Dacre of Mountmellick, Ireland, at the age of 16. At 18 she signed the coverlet with the initials 'M.D.', the figure 1, and the date '1827'. Margaret married a housepainter and went to live in Dublin in 1829 and in the ensuing years bore eleven children. The quilt of cream calico has been applied with chintzes, sewn to the ground with buttonhole stitch. Unlike most examples of Broderie Perse this bed-cover has been quilted with flowers, shells, diamonds and spirals. 8 ft × 9 ft (244 cm × 274 cm). (Ulster Folk and Transport Museum)

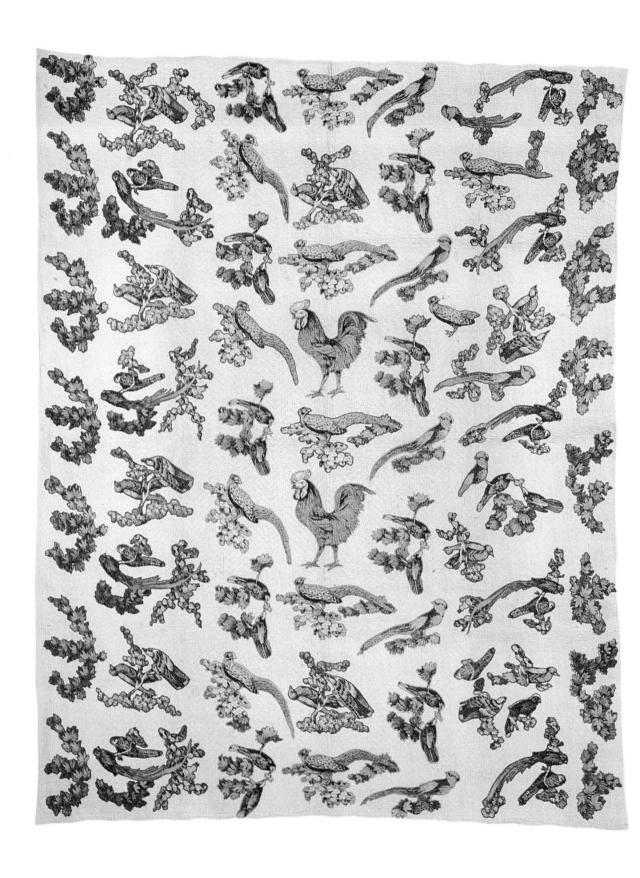

Game bird and foliage appliqué on white cotton twill background, which has been quilted with waves. Made in the nineteenth century. 5 ft 5 in × 6 ft 10 in (165 cm × 208 cm). (Ulster Folk and Transport Museum)

unusual, which is why the quilt on page 81 is rare. The quilt originated in Mountmellick, Queen's County, Ireland, and is dated 1827 and signed. (Mountmellick, a town known for its textiles, is also associated with heavy embroidery worked with knitting cotton on thick material.) The needlewoman who sewed this quilt was highly proficient in the art of Broderie Perse, which calls for a certain skill in grouping like objects – and she was also a quilter. Quilting was never a highly developed art in Ireland, yet the two layers of this cover (there is no filling) have been quilted in shells, diamonds and flowers. Another fine example of Broderie Perse is also shown in the work of the convict women who were being transported in 1841 (see page 112).

The subjects most commonly associated with Broderie Perse are floral, but other figurative prints were used: the game-bird quilt on page 82 is a good example. The fabric used here is a furnishing fabric, probably printed in the early nineteenth century, during the vogue in textile printing for game birds. The birds have been applied to the white ground with red thread and there is substantial quilting.

The Broderie Perse technique often employed paste as well as buttonhole or feather embroidery stitches to hold the cut pieces in place. There were also vague rules to observe, one being to avoid too great a contrast between the background and design and too lavish a use of brilliant flowers or birds. S.F.A. Caulfield gave these directions:

The worker should bear in mind that the setting of one or two brilliant colours among several subdued ones will produce a much better effect than the crowding together of a number of equally bright shades. Much will depend upon the selection of flowers, etc. The best come from old pieces of chintz manufactured before the days of aniline dyes; their shades mix together without offence, and their outlines are generally clear and decided. When not procurable, select bold single modern chintz or cretonne flowers of quiet tone and conventional design.

Sepia cock stitched to ground with red cotton.

Avoid bright colours, and choose citron, lemon, red, red-browns, lavenders, and cream-whites. Sunflowers, tulips, hollyhocks, crown imperials, foxgloves, chrysanthemums, peonies, sweet peas, anemones, thistles, are all good flowers. Palm leaves or Virginia creeper leaves make good designs alone, but not amalgamated, and ferns are not used at all.[6]

The project recommended in this instance was a Broderie Perse picture of storks and water plants. The cut-out flowers and leaves were to be initially grouped on a piece of white paper and an outline drawn around them. The background fabric was to be stretched on a frame or clothes horse, the outline of designs transferred to the background with carbon paper, and the pieces of cloth subsequently pasted. Once the paste was dry, the work was to be taken from the frame and embroidered. Satin stitch was recommended for added definition on the leaves and flowers and the plumage of the birds, crewel and long stitch for the grasses, and buttonhole stitches to apply the bird prints.

PRINTED CENTREPIECES

The early part of the nineteenth century also saw the production of printed medallions and borders in chintz. The medallions often required as many as twelve different blocks to print, but whether they were intended solely for use in quiltmaking is debatable. They were probably designed for use in soft furnishings, pillows or loose covers. The printed centrepieces were usually oval or eight-sided and often featured very stylized pictures of baskets of fruit or bouquets of flowers. They were sometimes referred to as Sheraton panels, no doubt because of the famous furniture designer's preference for inlay decoration and classical motifs.

A few of these centrepieces were commemorative. The marriage of Princess Charlotte Augusta, only child of George IV, provided one celebratory theme. Charlotte married Prince Leopold of Saxe-Coburg in 1816. The centrepiece of glazed cotton printed for the event depicts a central floral bouquet with a rose border and four royal motifs: the

Printed chintz centrepieces made in the early nineteenth
century. (The Castle Museum, York)

Irish frame quilt with brown and cream border prints made
in 1850. 7 ft 6 in × 9 ft 3 in (229 cm × 282 cm). (Ulster Folk
and Transport Museum)

Centre of appliquéd coverlet, made about 1820, commemorating the marriage of Princess Charlotte to Prince Leopold of Saxe-Coburg in 1816. 7 ft 8 in × 7 ft 10 in (234 cm × 239 cm). (The Castle Museum, York)

inscription reads 'Princess Charlotte of Wales Married to Leopold Prince of Saxecobourg May 2 1816'. Tragically, the marriage ended after only one year, the Princess dying in childbirth. A commemorative panel was also printed to mark the death of the British naval hero, Admiral Lord Nelson, at the Battle of Trafalgar on 21 October 1805, and another panel printed to commemorate the golden jubilee of George III in 1810.

Regardless of their original purpose, these panels obviously proved a good decorative focus for quiltmakers, who often just appliquéd these centres on to the middle of a bed-sized piece of linen and then finished the cover with other bits of appliqué or piecing. The quilt on this page has four of the Princess Charlotte panels surrounding a printed floral centre. Printed 'frame' borders separate the panels of Broderie Perse. The scrap quilt on page 33 features a printed portrait of Queen Caroline.

CHINTZ SCRAP APPLIQUÉ

The much prized chintz also appears in another type of appliqué which differs slightly from Broderie Perse. Instead of cutting out well-defined prints and applying them to a ground, needlewomen would apply scraps of chintz, sometimes in shapes like leaves and hearts. In this instance, little regard was paid to creating a new picture. The object seemed to be to use up chintz scraps, even if they were of no particular shape.

Two quilts of this description are in Scottish collections. One shown on page 87 has associations with the East India Company. The quilt came into the possession of the Highland Folk Museum at Kingussie through Mackintosh of Farr, a tacksman (a tenant) of Clan Mackintosh. The Farr family of Mackintoshes take their name from lands situated in the Inverness-shire parish of Daviot and Dunlichity, on the River Nairn about eight miles south of Inverness. A relative of the donor, Alexander Mackintosh of Farr (1790–1867) was in the service of the East India Company, which played such a famous part in the development of British fortunes in India and of course was also responsible for importing \Indian chintzes into Britain.

The second quilt is at Crathes Castle, Kincardineshire, the ancestral home of an ancient Scottish family, the Burnetts of Leys. The property is now owned by the National Trust for Scotland. The Crathes quilt is larger than the one in the Kingussie collection but identical in composition:

white linen strips have been appliquéd with chintz patches and then joined with Turkey Red panels. Both covers have been backed, but have no filling and are not quilted.

The quilt at Crathes Castle was made by Lauderdale Ramsay, Lady Burnett, and was completed by her in 1878 when she was seventy-two years of age. Lady Burnett, the second wife of the 10th Baronet, Sir James Horn Burnett, had been widowed two years earlier after thirty-nine years of marriage. She died in 1888 at the age of eighty-two.

Clearly, Lady Burnett regarded the quilt as a significant piece of work and wanted the rest of the family to recognize its worth. There is a handwritten inscription on the back of the quilt, in Indian ink. It reads:

This coverlet is worked entirely by Lauderdale Ramsay, Lady Burnett, is given by her to her grandnephew, Thomas Burnett Ramsay of Banchory Lodge, to be kept in remembrance of her as an heirloom for the family. 1878.

It is not known why Lady Burnett bequeathed the quilt to Thomas in particular, though it may be significant that he was aged sixteen at the time. Perhaps she felt he was the youngest member of the family old enough to appreciate the idea of family continuity. Thomas, who followed a military career, became a major in the Rifle Brigade. He died a bachelor in 1901 in South Africa, at the age of forty.

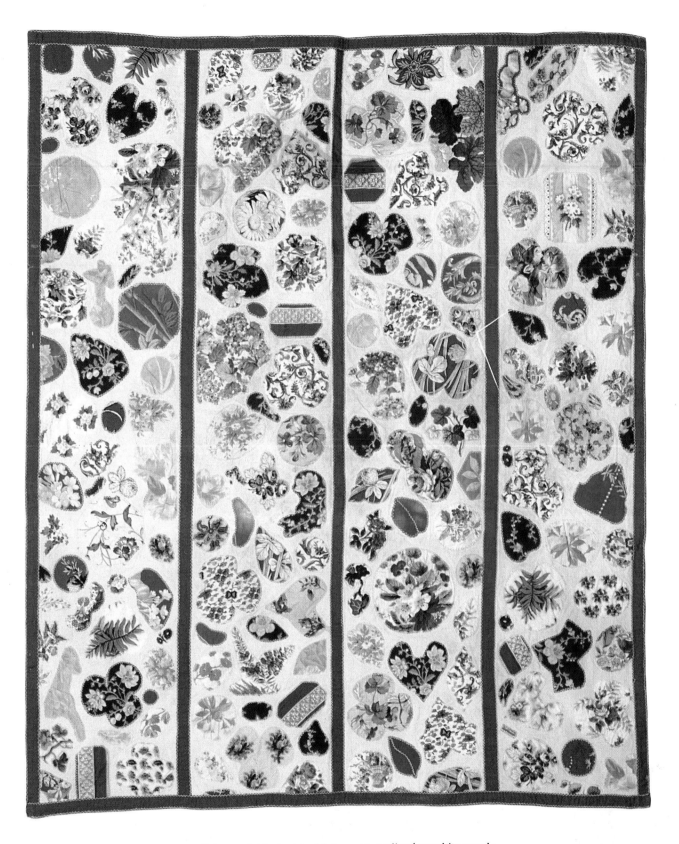

Cot coverlet featuring chintz scrap appliqué on white panels
joined with Turkey Red. There is no filling or quilting on this
coverlet, which was probably made in the second half of the
nineteenth century. 3 ft 5 in × 4 ft (104 cm × 122 cm).
(Highland Folk Museum)

PAPER-CUTTING

The nineteenth-century enthusiasm for Turkey Red plus a vogue for using paper-cutting techniques on fabric – the kind of folded paper-cutting that children are introduced to when making snowflake shapes – also resulted in a specific type of appliquéd quilt which appears in collections in Ireland and Wales. Inevitably, the cut-out was made from Turkey Red and applied to a white ground, and although there was a backing there was no quilting. Some of the shapes created by this method were very coarse; others were rather more delicate and required more skill in the application.

Hearts and birds appear frequently as motifs on the Irish quilts although there is no known significance for this. Often the quiltmaker would apply one cut-out shape as a medallion and then surround it with a collection of smaller and different shapes. This was done with quite a free hand and often with complete insensitivity to scale. Both hand- and machine-sewing techniques were used in the application and sometimes the edges were finished with a herringbone stitch.

Red cut-outs were also used to simulate block quilts. The Ulster Folk and Transport Museum collection has one whole cloth quilt with twenty identical cut-outs of oak leaves, which have all been applied in rows. A more complex pseudo-block quilt in red and white is to be found in Wales. There are nine panels, each containing an identical four-leaf flower cut-out. However, the panels alternate: in one a red flower has been laid on; in the adjoining panel a red square with the flower removed from it has been applied, thus giving the effect of a white flower with a red surround.

MIXED MEDIA

In the nineteenth century appliqué was also used frequently as a focal point in frame quilts, in combination with piecing. The convict quilt on page 111 has a Broderie Perse centre surrounded by pieced borders. The scrap quilt on page 93 demonstrates a variety of piecing patterns, set out in frames and an appliquéd centre which features a central flower and four hexagons.

These mixed media covers generally showed a great deal of ambition on the part of the maker, though not always an ability to achieve definitive artistry. In fact, one is driven to speculate that some were cut out by children. The figures which have been appliquéd on the medallion centre of the quilt shown below are a good example. Some imagination is needed to decipher some of the objects since all appear quite crude in execution. All are thought to be of a domestic nature, though one has to be familiar with the interior of a late nineteenth-century Irish home to be able to interpret them.

An earlier example, with the same kind of primitive cut-out shapes applied to a ground, can be found in the collection of the Dundee Museums and Art Galleries in Scotland. The objects chosen for appliqué include a very crude star in the centre of the cover and figures with joined hands. There are also cut-outs of hearts, diamonds, stars and animals. All the figures have been scattered on a white ground and appliquéd with a rough orange cross stitch and the cover has been finished with a white fringe. The quilt is known to have been made by Janet McLaggan about 1830. Part of a similar cover with primitive figures which have been crudely appliquéd in a running stitch, is also in the collection of the Ulster Folk and Transport Museum. The four-inch-high figures of men, women and geese, in mauve, blue, pink and brown cotton prints, are set in rows round a central star. The coverlet is from Swanlinbar and is believed to have been made about the middle of the nineteenth century. Unfortunately, only a section of the cover remains – the rest was eaten by a cow while hanging on a clothes line! In the instance of the Dundee coverlet, the printed cottons have faded and some are holed where brown dye has been used. This is due to the former practice of using iron in the dye.

Appliqué detail showing primitive cut-outs, including a spoon, a figure, a tea kettle and bellows.

Turkey Red appliqué on white cotton ground made of three
lengths of fabric handsewn together. The daisies, clover and
central medallion were fashioned with the folded paper-
cutting technique and applied with white cotton thread. The
coverlet, made in Northern Ireland in the second half of the
nineteenth century, is bound in red and backed but it is
neither filled nor quilted. 6 ft 6 in square (198 cm). (Ulster
Folk and Transport Museum)

Whole cloth quilt appliquéd with Turkey Red oak leaf and
circle cut-out. 5 ft 7 in × 7 ft (171 cm × 213 cm). (Ulster Folk
and Transport Museum)

Mauve and white pieced and appliquéd frame quilt with
windmill medallion centre. Flying Geese border on four sides
and zig-zag border on three sides. Backed with white cotton
twill and quilted in waves but unfilled. Made by Margaret
Waterson of Rathfriland, Ireland, about 1870. 6 ft 3 in × 7 ft
(191 cm × 213 cm). (Ulster Folk and Transport Museum)

Late nineteenth-century frame quilt with medallion of appliquéd red hearts and outer border of pieced sunbursts. Quilted in waves. 6 ft 3 in × 6 ft 10 in (191 cm × 208 cm). (Ulster Folk and Transport Museum)

Frame scrap quilt with appliquéd and pieced centre. A
number of dress fabrics have been used in this quilt, which is
linen backed and quilted in waves. Made in Omagh, County
Tyrone about 1860. 6 ft 7 in × 7 ft (201 cm × 213 cm).
(Ulster Folk and Transport Museum)

Inlay table cover in black, beige, and brown made in the late
nineteenth century in Machynlleth, Montgomery. 5 ft 4 in
square (163 cm). (Photograph courtesy of the Welsh Folk
Museum)

PICTURES IN CLOTH

One of the most exacting forms of patchwork made in Britain during the last part of the nineteenth century was that which resembled marquetry. Inlay patchwork, as opposed to appliqué, seems to have been the almost exclusive prerogative of tailors. It was figurative, made of heavy non-fraying uniform or suit cloth and embellished with embroidery. It resembled cloisonné enamel in that each piece usually had a chain stitch outline or gold couching. It has also been compared with Boulle work, a type of marquetry decoration invented and highly developed by the famous French cabinetmaker, André Charles Boulle (1642–1732). He incorporated, for example, brass and tortoiseshell in his inlays, and numbered Louis XIV among his illustrious clients.

Inlay patchwork demanded a high degree of skill and patience. It also called for something of an artistic eye, or at least the ability to be a good copyist. The technique is described thus:

The cloth to be inlaid is placed upon the other, and both are cut through with one action of the knife, so that parts cannot but fit. The coherent piece of material is then laid upon a piece of strong linen already in a frame; the vacant spaces in it are filled up by pieces of the other stuff, and all is tacked down in place. That done, the work is taken out of the frame and the edges sewn together. The backing can then, if necessary, be removed.[7]

The inlay technique required that fabric edges butt each other, and that the cloth used be thick enough to accommodate the oversewing required to hold the pieces in place. The oversewing was done from the back with very fine stitches which did not completely pierce the cloth, and the embroidery stitch was decorative rather than functional. Inlay, however, was also accomplished with the customary seam and running stitch. The floral table cover pictured opposite is a good example. Heavy felt-like cloth was used to make this cover and each of the flowers was actually 'dropped into' the background and seamed with a running stitch. Both the design and the technique, however, make this an unusual example of inlay.

The origins of inlay patchwork are to be found in Italy, Spain and the Middle East. What the British practitioners of this cloth craft did, however, was to borrow the technique for the reproduction of cloth pictures. Compared to appliqué, inlay offered greater opportunity for reproducing fine detail. Many of the picture hangings made by this method included reproductions of favourite prints, the prints themselves possibly being used as patterns.

Other picture hangings had definite historical links. In the Great Exhibition of 1851 in London, Stephen Stokes of Dublin exhibited a table cover of mosaic cloth-work, which included the royal arms; the royal family at a review; the capture of a French eagle by the Scots Greys at Waterloo; a sketch from Ballingarry; and a war chariot. He was listed in the Exhibition's catalogue as the 'inventor' of this piece of work – a suitable enough description in the circumstances.

The same exhibition also had a 'counterpane of mosaic needlework, 12 feet long by 10 feet wide, divided into 44 compartments, each representing a popular print, worked up of coloured pieces of cloth'. John Bradshaw of Lancaster was the 'producer' of this particular piece.

Several of these unusual examples of inlay patchwork have survived in museum collections. One, which looks more like a collage in composition than other examples, is that in the collection of the Welsh Folk Museum at St Fagans. It was made between 1842 and 1845 by James Williams, a tailor from Wrexham and it consists of biblical motifs, including Jonah and the whale, Noah's Ark, and Cain killing Abel, as well as the emblems of each of the four countries within the UK – the rose, the thistle, the shamrock and the leek. Curiously, the Menai suspension bridge constructed by Telford in 1826, and the Ruabon viaduct opened in 1828, are also included. The latter acts almost as a pictorial platform for the figure of Adam and a group of animals. One can only conclude that the tailor who made this particular hanging chose to depict the things he liked best.

The Kelvingrove Museum and Art Gallery in Glasgow have three such examples of inlay patchwork. Two are wall hangings by David Robertson of Falkirk. One, a picture of the American clipper, *Cobra*, was made by Robertson in 1859; his other hanging, shown on page 96, was worked in 1853 and took 1,650 hours to complete, a fact duly noted on the work.

The 'Royal Clothograph Work of Art' in the same collection is more complex. It took eighteen years to make and, following the death of its maker, John Monro, was raffled on behalf of his widow. The raffle took place on 8 March 1888 and the tickets were sold at one shilling (5p) each. This hanging is made of uniform material and there are altogether seven scenes, which look as though they could have been copied from prints. Each scene is surrounded by a border made up of triangles, and the number of

Inlay patchwork hanging made by David Robertson of Falkirk, Stirlingshire, in 1853. A ship occupies the centre panel and a number of prints have been reproduced in cloth around two edges. The emblem of the lion and unicorn at the top carries the phrase 'Dieu et Mon Droit'. Robertson spent 1,650 hours on this piece of work. 8ft 6in×8ft 11in (259×272cm). (Glasgow Museums and Art Galleries)

The 'Royal Clothograph' worked by John Monro, a Paisley artist/tailor who was born in 1811. In addition to the pictures, Monro has embroidered the names of famous and intellectual men around the border as well as the following guidance: 'To Gain the Grand End. We ought to keep in Mind 7 words. 1st Push 2nd Piety 3rd Patience 4th Perseverance 5th Punctuality 6th Penetrate 7th Please. Stop. Man Know Thyself and others learn to know. Love God and Man. Amen.' 6 ft 7 in square (201 cm). (Glasgow Museums and Art Galleries)

Scene from the Royal
Clothograph.

pieces in each picture is recorded in embroidery. It is the forthright opinions of the maker, however, that add character to the piece. Monro obviously held Scotland's national bard, Robert Burns, in high esteem, for he equates the poet with the British Lion: the picture of the lion is labelled 'Burns'. Monro embroidered the names of 'Men of Learning' round the border of his work, including such diverse figures as Livingstone, Wellington, Bonaparte, Ramsay, Boswell, Wallace and (somewhat out of gender) 'Victoria'. He has also added a few of his own thoughts in embroidery lettering (see page 97).

An even more remarkable example of inlay patchwork is in the collection of the Biggar Museums Trust in Lanarkshire. It was worked by Menzies Moffat, sometime photographer, tailor and local eccentric who had artistic aspirations. He died about 1908, and but for the fact that he was penniless and living on local charity, the table cover would have been lost for ever. Moffat had expressed the desire to be buried in it, but because the parish was paying for the funeral his wish was denied.

The work by Menzies Moffat was inspired by a number of contemporary prints. It has equestrian figures of Crimean leaders, medallions of Queen Victoria and the Prince Consort, and contemporary theatrical figures to name but a few – some eighty-one figures in the work have been identified as relating to prints.[8] It measures some eight feet by ten feet and is permanently on display, under glass, in one of the town's historic buildings.

VICTORIAN EXCESSES

Appliqué in the hands of the Victorians became something of an absurdity, especially the practice of appliquing or embroidering on individual pieces used to make crazy patchwork. One writer has described the development of the crazy quilt in the 1880s as 'the supreme efflorescence of tastelessness'.[9] Crazy quilts, which were also referred to as 'Japanese patchwork' or 'Kaleidoscope', did provide, however, a cogent social record of the times in the same way as did family scrapbooks. The cut-outs that were appliquéd usually recorded domestic trivia: pets like cats and dogs, birds and rabbits; items of apparel such as top hats and ladies' fans; or

Appliquéd cover made by Mr and Mrs Bellamy of Yarmouth, to illustrate memorabilia and interests in their lives. All of the objects have been appliquéd to panels, with the spaces between filled with gold stem stitch. The border of blue velvet has a bobble edging and the back is yellow and quilted. Made in 1891. 6 ft square (183 cm). (Strangers' Hall, Norfolk Museums Service)

Right: Detail of appliquéd quilt showing Queen Victoria and Prince Albert.

Far right: Taffeta quilt with appliquéd and padded vase of flowers. Embellished with embroidery and bead work. Made in 1860. 6 ft 2 in × 7 ft (188 cm × 213 cm). (Strangers' Hall, Norfolk Museums Service)

household utensils like scissors, candlesticks, cups and the like. The scraps that were used were also a record of sorts, since crazy patchwork required luxury fabrics like velvets, silks and satins and ribbons – the pieces left from dressmaking.

The quilt which demonstrates Victorian appliqué at its zenith (though it is not crazy patchwork, but strips of appliqué), is pictured on page 99. Sewing the many pieces of appliqué to the background of this quilt must have occupied many a long winter evening. The choice of subjects not only catalogues milestones in the life of the husband and wife who worked on the luxury cover, but a sense of humour. A number of comic figures and greeting card

designs are included, as well as figures of Prince Albert and Queen Victoria, which are decorated with sequins. So too is the phrase 'Nil Desperandum' – perhaps embroidered as a comment upon the long hours of needle activity or perhaps upon the burdens of everyday life. There are a number of features which make this particular example of appliqué unusual. It is more than simply pieces of shaped fabric stitched to a ground and embellished with embroidery; there are some bits of canvas work as well. More unusual is the fact that the yellow ground is actually row upon row of stem stitch, which has been used as a fill between the appliquéd figures.

ART NEEDLEWORK

It is small wonder that the affluent ostentation in textile decoration practised by the Victorians was followed by a reaction. The two developments that had the greatest impact on needlework of any description from 1876 onwards were the establishment of the Royal School of Art Needlework in London and the Arts and Crafts

Movement which advocated a return to simplicity and nature.

The Royal School had been started in premises over a bonnet shop in Sloane Street with the aim of restoring ornamental needlework to the place it had formerly held in decorative art. Its attention was turned towards the reproduction of historic embroideries, repairs and exquisite stitchery rather than innovation. The school had an active royal patron in the person of Princess Christian of Schleswig-Holstein, Queen Victoria's third daughter, and it had another energetic supporter in the person of Lady Marian Alford, whose book, *Needlework as Art,* published in 1886, became a standard work of reference. Lady Alford became vice-president of the school.

The school provided lessons as well as employment and in order to be considered eligible for admission, applicants had to be 'gentlewomen by birth and education' and 'able and willing when employed to devote seven hours a day to working at the school'.[10] They also had to have at least one reference from a clergyman. The course at the school cost five pounds and consisted of nine lessons in art needlework, each of which was five hours in length. Women who successfully completed the course and worked at the school – and by 1883 there were about 120 employed there – were expected to be able to produce stitches and designs from any period in history – Gothic, Renaissance, Elizabethan, James I or Queen Anne. Their pay was between twenty and thirty shillings (£1 to £1.50) a week.

The success of the Royal School launched 'art needlework' as a movement and the term became widespread. Art neeedlework in terms of quiltmaking is best illustrated by the description of a quilt made in 1888 to mark the silver wedding of the Princess of Wales (the Danish Princess, Alexandra, wife of Prince Edward, who succeeded his mother, Queen Victoria, in 1901). The quilt, which was designed and mounted by the Decorative Needlework Society and made by about twenty ladies from Radnorshire who worked the quilt in sections, had 'a background of cream-coloured brocade, which has a small pattern all over it; and embroidery executed with floss silk and outlined with silver'.[11] Embroidering on top of brocade or damask was a fashionable technique at the time and the royal quilt had an excess of stitchery. The centre medallion, which contained the royal monogram, was surrounded by a field of scroll work and an outer border of closely worked embroidery which featured gigantic thistles in each of the four corners. A small inner border recording the silver wedding also bears the dates 1863 and 1888 and the inscription 'From the ladies of Radnorshire'.

Art needlework entered the homes of ordinary needlewomen through a number of books and periodicals at the end of the nineteenth and into the early twentieth century. Lewis Day, a prolific writer on ornament and decorations (his other books were on stained glass, old and new alphabets and 'nature in ornament'), was one of the more opinionated:

Appliqué work is thought by some to be an inferior kind of embroidery, which it is not. It is not a lower but another kind of needlework, in which more is made of the stuff than of the stitching. In it the craft of the needleworker is not carried to its limit; but, on the other hand, it makes great demands upon design. You cannot begin by just throwing about sprays of natural flowers. It calls peremptorily for treatment – by which test the decorative artist stands or falls. Effective it must be; coarse it may be; vulgar it should not be; trivial it can hardly be; mere prettiness is beyond its scope; and it lends itself to dignity of design and nobility of treatment. Of course, it is not popular.[12]

The same author had little regard for the designing abilities of women, indicating that such things were best left to the men: 'Embroidery proper is properly woman's work; but here, as in the case of tailoring, the man comes in. The getting ready for appliqué is not the kind of thing a woman can do best.'[13]

The Arts and Crafts Movement also influenced needlework. Quiltmaking was not practised in the traditional sense, but there was much use of appliqué and embroidery for domestic items, including coverlets. The influence of the Movement on quiltmaking has to be considered not only because it heralded the end of the rich Victorian parlour quilt or table cover, but because it changed attitudes towards colour, fabric and, most important, design. Experiments in appliqué made by M.H. Baillie Scott in the late nineteenth century give an indication of the new emphasis on simplicity. Scott was an architect who designed a number of articles, including bed-covers. 'In appliqué work,' he said, 'it seems important that the applied pieces should be as large as may be and as simple in outline as possible. The method loses its reasonableness as soon as the pieces become small.'[14] Scott used invisible thread and what he described as 'peasant embroidery probably because it is seldom practised by peasants and cannot be strictly described as embroidery'. By peasant embroidery he meant the outlining of the pieces of appliqué in imitation of the lead in stained glass windows – he preferred grey thread for this purpose.

GLASGOW STYLE

The real challenge to the teaching of the Royal School in London, however, came from Glasgow and from Jessie Rowat Newbery and Ann Macbeth. Both were associated with the Glasgow School of Art and its emergence into the international arena as the originator of the 'Glasgow Style' – a style which proved quite unlike any other. Perhaps the best known figure connected with this movement is Charles Rennie Mackintosh, the furniture and interior designer and architect.

Jessie Rowat, who had studied drawing, stained glass and textiles at the Glasgow School of Art, conducted the school's first embroidery class in 1894, some five years before she married Francis or 'Fra' Newbery, the school's energetic and influential director. Everything about her needlework was original.

> She [Jessie Newbery] rebelled against embroidery in which the colours used were predominantly dark, the design often stereotyped and the quality of the work judged solely on the intricacies of the stitchwork. In her embroidery class, Jessie Newbery encouraged individuality and originality in design. She also introduced new colour schemes, new materials and stressed that complicated stitches were not necessarily the criterion of a fine embroideress.[15]

Mrs Newbery's successor at Glasgow was Ann Macbeth, a talented and prize-winning pupil of the school whose influence was felt much further afield. Ann Macbeth contributed to and wrote a number of books on needle crafts, including *Embroidered Lace and Leatherwork, The Countrywoman's Rug Book* and *Needleweaving*. She also co-authored the influential *Educational Needlecraft*, published in 1911, which was widely adopted by sewing teachers in the UK and also in New Zealand, Australia, Canada, India and the United States.

In writing the foreword to a book by another author, Ann Macbeth expressed her low regard for the embroidery of the time:

> To be in a healthy and living state, our art should be constantly changing its fashion; if it stands still, it is retrograde, and for some few generations we may say this of British embroidery. What changes it has undergone are due almost entirely to the commercial enterprise of manufacturers of printed patterns – usually foreign ones. The importation became very considerable with the introduction of so-called Berlin woolwork, and since that period the British needlewoman has set aside her own ingenious arrangements and follows blindly where the merchant leads, and British design for needlework, as an expression of its people, is almost a dead thing.[16]

Appliqué was a very important decorative feature of the Glasgow Style embroidery. Popular colours were greys, silvers and lilacs, as well as black and white, and the most popular fabric was linen. Needleweaving, the technique of removing either the warp or weft threads of a fabric and working a pattern through the remaining threads, was often used as a border outline. The object most associated with Glasgow work is the elongated stylized rose motif, although rondels of flowers were also used (see the cover on the left). Another feature of Glasgow Style embroidery was lettering. One

Centre of a coverlet which shows the influence of Jessie Newbery. Made by Mary Duncan, a student at the Glasgow School of Art, in the late 1890s. 5 ft 2 in × 7 ft 4 in (157 cm × 224 cm). (Glasgow Museums and Art Galleries)

unfinished coverlet in the Mackintosh Collection belonging to the Glasgow School of Art, believed to have been made by a student of Jessie Newbery about 1900, is a mix of appliquéd hearts on beige linen, with needleweaving as a border detail, and a centre medallion containing a verse:

God Knows and
What He Knows
is Well and Best
The Darkness
Hideth Not from
Him but Glows
Clears as the
Morning or the
Evening Rose
of East or West.

The Glasgow Style made frequent use of Celtic motifs, a fact which may have had some influence on a quilt of applied work which was featured in the October 1914 issue of *Needle and Thread,* a London periodical. A dark blue linen ground was applied with a mass of interlacing Celtic knots and circles in pale blue, yellow and white. These had been applied with narrow braid-like tape dyed to match the colours of linen used and couched round the raw edges of the interlacing knots. The technique, which has found renewed favour with contemporary quiltmakers, is now known as Celtic appliqué.

This was certainly one of the most complicated uses of appliqué to be used in connection with quiltmaking in the early part of the twentieth century. Although appliqué continued to be used as a needlework technique for many household items like table cloths and tea towels, into the 1930s and beyond, quiltmaking when undertaken reverted in the main to piecing and quilting.

Notes

1. Mary Gostelow, *Embroidery Book,* London: Penguin Books, 1982.
2. Margaret Swain, *Scottish Embroidery,* London, 1986.
3. A more complete explanation can be found in *Origins of Chintz* by John Irwin and Katharine Brett, London, 1970.
4. Ibid.
5. Catalogue, SWRI Exhibition of Needlework, Royal Scottish Academy, 1934.
6. S.F.A. Caulfield, *The Dictionary of Needlework,* London, 1887, p.10.
7. Lewis F. Day, *Art in Needlework,* London, 1900, p.153.
8. Margaret Swain, *Figures on Fabric,* London, 1980, pp.72–8.
9. Frances Lichten, *Decorative Art of Victoria's Era,* London, 1950.
10. Mercy Grogan, *How Women May Earn a Living,* London: Cassell, 1883.
11. Ellen T. Masters, *The Gentlewoman's Book of Art Needlework,* London, 1893, p.61.
12. Day, op cit., p.148.
13. Ibid., p.145.
14. M.H. Baillie Scott, 'Some Experiments in Embroidery', *The Studio,* Vol. 18, 1903.
15. Fiona C. Macfarlane and Elizabeth F. Arthur, *Glasgow School of Art Embroidery 1894–1920,* Glasgow, 1980.
16. Ann Macbeth, Foreword to *An Embroidery Book* by Anne Knox Arthur, London, 1920, p.vii.

5

ONE OF A KIND

Some quilts are so singular that they deserve a special niche in needlework history, either because of their makers or because of the circumstances surrounding their creation. Commemorative bed-covers are a good example – especially the finely quilted whole cloth marriage quilts which have survived in Welsh collections – or quilts which have been made by families or groups. The ladies of the Ince family of Acton must have spent many companionable hours in the early nineteenth century translating their favourite Bible stories into appliqué. The bed-cover they made was not only pieced, it was appliquéd with four scenes: Christ and the woman of Samaria, Elijah and the ravens, Christ giving sight to a blind man and Elijah and the poor widow.[1]

Another family project was that undertaken by the Davis family of Liverpool, who celebrated Queen Victoria's golden jubilee in 1887 by piecing taffeta, velvet, brocade and silk into eight-pointed stars and incorporating woven red silk jubilee ribbon with a crown and the royal coat of arms. The four square blocks at the centre of the quilt bear the initials of the various family members.[2]

AUTOGRAPH QUILTS

Signature of Neddy Scrymgeour, who unseated Winston Churchill in the 1922 general election.

Quilts that have been signed by their makers are rare. So too are autograph quilts, coverlets or portières that bear the signatures of the famous reproduced in embroidery. Of particular historical interest, then, is the Prohibitionists' Autograph Portière (1904) in the collection of the Dundee Museums and Art Galleries.

A portière, strictly speaking, is a door-curtain, but this impressive expanse of satin piecing was probably used as a party banner. There are weather stains on some of the satin squares which suggest that the portière, with its slogan 'Vote as you pray', was probably displayed at outdoor meetings (see page 105).

The portière contains autographs of members of the Scottish Prohibition Party, including that of Edwin (Neddy) Scrymgeour. It also immortalizes a famous episode in British political history. Neddy Scrymgeour, a native of Dundee, was an upright and sincere man whose mission in life was to persuade others that the total abolition of the liquor trade was essential to a better world. He was a devoted socialist from a Methodist family, and in 1901, at the age of thirty-five, he founded the Scottish Prohibition Party in Dundee. Scrymgeour was elected to Dundee Town Council, and in 1908

104

'Vote As You Pray.' The 1904 Prohibitionists' Autograph Portiere, made of brightly coloured satin blocks embroidered with the signatures of party members. 6 ft 7 in × 6 ft 10 in (201 cm × 208 cm). (City of Dundee Museums and Art Galleries)

he stood for Parliament against a certain Winston Churchill, young, brilliant and already famous. Churchill won the seat easily while Neddy Scrymgeour polled a mere 655 votes and lost his deposit.

Undeterred, Scrymgeour kept coming back at subsequent parliamentary elections until, in the general election of 1922, he unseated Churchill and won the seat for the Prohibition Party. He was returned to Parliament on three more occasions before being defeated in 1931. He died, at the age of eighty, in 1947.

BAZAAR QUILTS

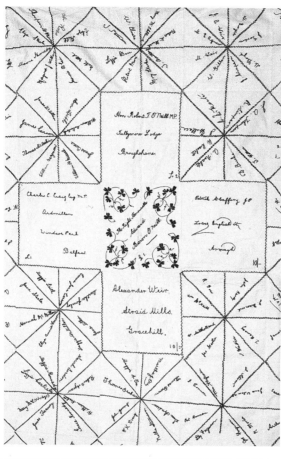

Right: Centre of Irish Bazaar coverlet. Red embroidery on white cotton and unbacked. 7 ft 9 in × 8 ft 6 in (238 cm × 258 cm). (Ulster Folk and Transport Museum)

Below: corner of Turkey Red and white star Bazaar coverlet made to benefit St John's School, Dewsbury, in 1892. 7 ft 3 in × 8 ft 5 in (221 cm × 257 cm). (The Castle Museum, York)

One curious practice that developed in the nineteenth century was the patchwork Bazaar or Signature coverlet, usually made in Turkey Red and white cotton. Although these did not carry reproduced signatures, they did include the names of people who had donated money to a particular charity or event, often with the amount of their donation included. The most generous donor to one such coverlet in the collection of the Ulster Folk and Transport Museum at Holywood, was the Right Honourable Edward, Baron O'Neill. His contribution of five pounds won him the centre square. Not only was his name and the amount of his donation embroidered in red, his square was embellished with flowers – unlike the squares allotted to Charles C. Craig, Esq., MP and the Hon. Robert T. O'Neill, MP, who had given only one pound and two pounds respectively.

The identification of two of the contributors as Members of Parliament enables us to date this quilt fairly precisely; it must have been completed at some time between 1903 and 1910. Charles Curtis Craig had been elected for the South Antrim constituency in 1903, and though he continued to serve in Parliament for a quarter of a century, we also know that his fellow MP, the Hon. Robert T. O'Neill, died in 1910.

Robert T. O'Neill, who must have been about sixty when he made his contribution to the quiltmakers, was the youngest brother of the third benefactor named, Edward, the 2nd Baron O'Neill. Edward, before succeeding to the title on the death of his father, had represented County Antrim in the British Parliament (1863–80). Baron O'Neill died in his eighty-ninth year, and his colleague Charles Craig lived to within a few weeks of his ninety-first birthday.

Many of these red and white coverlets were made to raise money for a church or a specific charity. The red and white star coverlet made at Dewsbury, Yorkshire, for the St John's School Bazaar in 1892, raised the sum of £10. 12s 6d (£10. 62½p). All of the stitching is by machine, including the names of the people who donated to the coverlet (see left). Another Bazaar coverlet in the collection at

106

Holywood was made specifically to raise money for the Zenana Mission in India. The wives of early missionaries to India had set about trying to improve the lives of Indian women living in seclusion and the coverlet made for the sale in Carnmoney documented this effort. The red and white cotton squares have been embroidered in red and light blue in crude stem stitch, and some of the squares are inscribed with first names like Flora and Fanny – even with nicknames like 'Buffalo Bill'. The pieced triangles down the side of the coverlet carry the explanation, 'WOMAN'S WORK' and 'IN INDIA A.D.V.' while the bottom border states: 'Presented by Sarah Ann Campbell. Paisley. Mossley, 14th Dec. 1887.'

BIBLE QUILTS

Bible, Scripture and Hymn quilts are another curiosity found in British textile collections. Sometimes they were called Hospital quilts. According to the Very Rev. Daniel Rock, writing in 1876, there was a quilt with the four Evangelists in the corners, on a bed in a priory dormitory in Durham in 1446. He also commented on the frequent practice of embroidering the figures of evangelists on children's cot-covers, 'reminding us of a nursery rhyme once common in England and abroad: "Matthew, Mark, Luke and John,/Bless the bed that I lie on." '[3]

S.F.A. Caulfield's *The Dictionary of Needlework* also mentions patchwork 'Hospital or Scripture' quilts on which Scriptural texts have either been written in ink or embroidered. Obviously a bit more care and time was taken in the making of these bed-covers than in some other charitable sewing: 'Quilts of Paper are much used for charitable purposes, as the material they are made of is very insusceptible to atmospheric influences, and promotes warmth by retaining heat.'[4] The paper quilts were puff patchwork, each four-inch square of chintz or 'old silk' being sewn on three sides, then stuffed with shredded paper and the individual square bags sewn together.

Three years after the second edition of the *Dictionary* was published, the Religious Tract Society in London issued a book for girls on *How to Make Common Things*.

Many Scripture quilts have been made and sent to various hospitals, both at home and, during war-time, to other countries, the aim, of course, being to set before the sick and suffering the Word of God, when they may be unable or unwilling to open the Bible for themselves.[5]

The directions for making a Scripture quilt were quite precise: the quilt pattern itself was utilitarian, being pieced of squares and rectangles of scraps. The important feature was the texts, all of which were required to be placed in a readable direction. Nine of the text blocks, including 'The wages of sin is death' and 'Blessed are the pure in heart for they shall see GOD' had to face the head of the bed in order that they could be read by the occupant.

Three remaining texts – including 'The blood of Jesus Christ cleanseth us from all sin' – were meant to be read by patients in beds on either side or visitors to the ward, for they all faced outwards.

Girls undertaking the making of a Scripture quilt were advised to use strong linen sheeting for the textual blocks since they provided the best surface on which to draw the letters. 'Do not attempt any other type than the plain letters, for which any printed book will furnish you a copy. Remember they must be very distinct.'[6] Scarlet or violet wool worked in chain stitch was recommended for the embroidery and a caution was given against using cretonnes for the patchwork pieces since the materials had to be washable. A strong calico lining was recommended but no filling, and it was also suggested that 'Floral borders and interlaced rings, with other designs which can easily be taken from the Berlin patterns, will make the quilt an object of interest, when the state of the patient can be benefited by something to attract attention'.[7]

Evidence exists which suggests it was also common to make coverlets with squares of religious texts which had been printed: the texts were probably mass-produced for embroidery samplers or other purposes. Leicestershire Museum has one such coverlet in its collection believed to date from

Centre panel of Bible quilt.

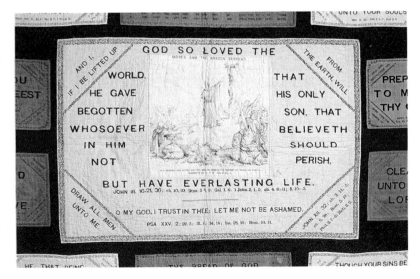

Bible quilt, composed of printed texts which have been machine appliquéd to Turkey Red twill. The quilting is rough and utilitarian, but the panel bearing the words and music of the hymn 'The Ascension' has been wave quilted. Made about 1860-80. 6 ft 7 in × 7 ft 1 in (201 cm × 216 cm). (Beamish North of England Open Air Museum)

Ann Johnson of Hartlepool was seventy-eight when she embroidered the flower blocks and eight verses of her favourite hymn, 'Jesu Lover of My Soul', round the border of this quilt. All of the blocks are satin and some have been pieced. The quilt is filled with wool and backed with cotton sateen. Made in 1885. 6 ft 9 in × 7 ft 1 in (206 cm × 216 cm).
(Beamish North of England Open Air Museum)

Ann Johnson's signature on the quilt border.

the late nineteenth century and to have been made by two elderly ladies in Rutland. The squares are machined together but have not been embroidered. Another is in the collection of Beamish North of England Open Air Museum (see pages 107 and 108).

In Scotland two Bible quilts dating from the latter part of the nineteenth century have a known religious affiliation. Both originated in the Highlands in areas where adherents of the Free Church of Scotland were congregated, following the break with the established Church of Scotland in 1843. One quilt, in the collection of the Auchindrain Museum near Inveraray, was obviously made by a group. The texts embroidered on the alternate red and white squares are stitched in a number of different styles of lettering: cursive, Gothic and Roman characters have all been employed, and with an indiscriminate use of upper and lower case. The text 'God is Love' appears more than once, but other texts include 'Christ died for the ungodly', 'Trust in the Lord', 'Seek ye the Lord', 'Be vigilant (2 Cor.v. viii)'. In fact, the last exhortation is found at 1 Peter 5. viii, not 2 Corinthians 5. viii (which welcomes an immortal life in heaven). The quotation is either a slip on the embroiderer's part, or she is offering some sound advice that has general application. This particular piece of work is believed to have been completed about 1850, at a time when the evangelical fervour of the Free Church was at a peak. The Gairloch Heritage Museum in Ross-shire also has a Bible quilt – this with a slightly macabre feel about it. All of the chosen texts have to do with 'rest', which, except for the cheerful colour might lead one to believe it had been used to cover a coffin. The centre panel of the red and white coverlet is a clock with Roman numerals and the phrases 'God is Love' and 'Love is of God'. The name of Jessie M. Finlay is embroidered across the clock face and the hands of the clock are at seven. This coverlet was also made by a group but this one is signed: a number of names appear on different blocks. (The mourning bed, with black drapes, coverlet and even sheets, figures in seventeenth-century British history but the black and white mourning quilt is generally unknown in Britain. The Irish used plain white coverlets for laying out the dead and the sole report of a black cot quilt made in Wales in the last century may be a reflection on the high infant mortality of the time or simply a matter of economy – perhaps black flannel was the only material at hand when the quilter sat down to work.)

The real contrast between Scripture or Bible quilts made from religious conviction, and those made perhaps for a charitable object, can be found in the work of middle-class Victorian needlewomen who had access to luxury fabrics and a surfeit of time in which to practise the art of embellishment. A good example of this is the extraordinary velvet table cover with rows of overlapping clam shells, which has been decorated with the verses of a hymn in crystal beads (see page 73). Another slightly less ornate version of a Hymn quilt was that made by Ann Johnson of Hartlepool, who was aged seventy-eight in 1885, which is presumably when the quilt was made. She has embroidered eight verses of her favourite hymn – 'Jesu Lover of my Soul' – on the black satin border of her quilt, while the centre medallion of squares and triangles is embroidered with: 'Endureth Forever'; 'God is Love'; 'Praise Ye the Lord'; and 'For His Mercy' (see page 109).

ELIZABETH FRY

The making of quilts to raise money or as appreciative gifts is an old practice which continues to the present day. Parishioners of the church in Husbands Bosworth, Leicestershire, made a parting quilt for their minister in 1895, which followed the style of many of the Bazaar quilts – pink and white squares embroidered with the parishioners' initials.[8] Similarly, a group of women herring workers on Scotland's North-East coast made a Log Cabin quilt in 1870 as a gift to one of their benefactors.[9] One of the great examples of quilt folklore in Britain, however, concerns the sewing of quilts in connection with both prison reform and transportation to the colonies. The story is well documented and fortunately some of the quilts made still survive. Elizabeth Fry, one of the diligent Quaker reformers of the early nineteenth century, who today would have been described as something of a 'superwoman', was the person responsible.

Elizabeth Gurney Fry was born in Norwich on 21 May 1780. Her parents were Quakers and her mother was a descendant of Robert Barclay the Apologist. Elizabeth was one of seven daughters born into the Gurney family and her good works began at an early age. One of her first charitable endeavours was to gather together seventy of Norwich's poorest children to teach – they became known as 'Betsy's Imps'.[10] At the age of twenty she married Joesph Fry and moved to London, where the next few years obviously were spent in domesticity and childbearing – she had eleven children in total.

In 1813, on hearing of the plight of women in London's Newgate Prison, Elizabeth Fry and a friend gathered together some clothing and went to the prison, where they discovered 300 women, with their numerous children, herded into four rooms. The conditions were appalling and the women were filthy. In the same cells were untried women accused of trivial offences and women convicted of atrocious crimes. Fortune-telling, card playing, drinking and swearing were the favourite pastimes. Somehow the two Quaker women managed to assemble the women together and conduct a short prayer meeting. After distributing the clothing, Elizabeth Fry and her friend left, promising to return.

Three years were to pass before Elizabeth Fry could begin her work of prison reform. When she did return to Newgate her first achievement was to set up within the prison a school for the under twenty-fives. One of the first teachers was Mary Connor, a prisoner who had been convicted of stealing a watch. In 1817, eleven members of the Society of Friends formed 'An Association for the Improvement of the Female Prisoners in Newgate' with the object of providing clothing, instruction and employment and introducing the prisoners to the Holy Scriptures.

The Quakers introduced democracy into the reform programme. Elizabeth Fry recorded in her own journal that the rules of the Association had been put to a vote. These included:

(1) that a matron be appointed for the general superintendence of the women; (2) that the women be engaged in needlework, knitting or any other suitable employment; (3) that there be no begging, swearing, gaming, card-playing, quarrelling or immoral conversation. That all novels, plays and other improper books be excluded; and that all bad words be avoided; and any default in these particulars be reported to the matron.[11]

Patchwork coverlets were sewn by the women inmates along with other domestic items, some of which ended up in sales of work organized by the Association. One such coverlet, believed to have been made in Newgate, is in the collection of Strangers' Hall in Norwich. It is a white piece of whole cloth on to which has been appliquéd a scattering of hexagon flowers. The centre is one large hexagon outline formed of hexagon scraps and the border consists of two rows of hexagon pieces.

Elizabeth Fry's work in Newgate led her to become interested in the women convicts sentenced to transportation and she began visiting ships making ready to sail for the colonies. There is some discrepancy about the origin of the idea that

Centre panel of pieced and Broderie Perse and appliqué coverlet, worked by convict women being transported to Tasmania. The central square is surrounded by twelve borders. Eight are pieced in triangles or squares and two are lengths of print. The outer border is appliqué and Broderie Perse. Made in 1841. 10 ft 6 in × 11 ft (320 cm × 335 cm). (Private collection)

To the Ladies
of the
Convict ship Committee
This quilt worked by the Convicts
of the Ship Rajah during their voyage
to Van Diemans Land is presented as a
testimony of the gratitude with which
they remember their exertions for their
welfare while in England and during
their passage and also as a proof that
they have not neglected the Ladies
kind admonitions of being industrious
· June · 1 8 4 1 ·

Explanatory note about the origins of the convicts' work embroidered in the coverlet's outside border. Van Diemens Land was the first name of the island of Tasmania, now part of Australia.

After Elizabeth Fry's death in 1843, her family received a letter and the gift of a calabash (gourd) from the garden of one of the women transported in 1823 aboard the *Brothers*. The woman had been one of the former schoolmistresses in Newgate, and recalled that when she set sail Mrs Fry had given her a pound of lump sugar and half a pound of tea. The two Fry daughters who edited their mother's journals duly recorded the successful status of the former prisoner:

Hester — has been married twenty years in New South Wales, is very comfortably established; and wished her former benefactress to be informed that she has 'plenty of pigs and fowls, buys her tea by the chest; and that the patchwork quilt which now covers her bed, was made of the pieces given her by the ladies when she embarked'.[12]

quilts be made on board ship during the voyage; one account gives credit to Elizabeth Fry and another to the captain of one of the ships. Whatever the truth, it is a fact that quilts were pieced on board these ships from scraps that had been provided to the prisoners by 'The British Ladies' Society for the Reformation of Female Prisoners'. One such quilt is shown on page 111. This group took a particular interest in the welfare of women prisoners and members would regularly visit departing convict ships, dispensing gifts of tea and other modest comforts.

Originally the sewing of quilts on board ship was intended as a profit-making venture and one which would also provide some industrious activity to relieve long hours of tedium. Arrangements were even made by the Quakers for the sale of these quilts in New South Wales, the proceeds being shared among the makers on landing. Some of the women convicts, however, held on to these bits of sewing: a coverlet of some description would have been a valuable practical possession for women arriving in Australia with only the clothes they wore.

Elizabeth Fry's interest in the ship in which Hester sailed went beyond the dispensing of comforts. Her prison reform work, which in her lifetime took her on visits to prisons and hospitals in Ireland, Scotland, France, Holland, Germany and Denmark, was then concentrated on the practice of shackling. When she visited the departing *Brothers* in 1823, it was to make a list of the names of those women who had arrived at the port in irons, so that a representation could be made to the government. From the list made at the time, it appears that twelve women arrived on board handcuffed; and eleven women from Lancaster were sent to the ship with iron hoops around their legs and arms, all chained to each other and some carrying children. One even more unfortunate soul from Cardigan on this occasion told Elizabeth Fry about being imprisoned with iron hoops around her waist, above the knee and around the ankle, all the hoops being joined by chains. Hester is not mentioned by name in the inventory but, since she was in Newgate, it can be deduced that she arrived at the ship in handcuffs.

SOLDIERS' AND SAILORS' QUILTS

Patchwork was also an activity undertaken very competently by men in the late 1800s – usually soldiers. Uniform or Soldiers' quilts, generally very geometric in concept, are made of hundreds of tiny squares of uniform fabric which, though heavy and lacking the flexibility of cotton, are nevertheless colourful, thanks to the variety of British regimental uniforms of the last century. The adoption of khaki subsequently made such a repertoire of colour impossible. A number of items of needlework,

including pieces of tapestry, wool work and patchwork, were shown in the Royal Military Exhibition of 1890 at the Royal Hospital in Chelsea, in aid of the Church of England Soldiers' Institutes.

Among soldiers, part of the attraction of sewing patchwork, aside from the fact that it filled in idle hours and provided warm covering, must have been the challenge of numbers – seeing how many tiny pieces of uniform fabric could be united in one cover. It was obviously a matter of pride for Lance

Late nineteenth-century soldier's quilt left by itinerant farm worker and former soldier with one of his employers in Northern Ireland. The quilt was originally backed with blue wool but this was destroyed by the farmer's children, who played with the quilt. 4 ft 10 in × 6 ft 6 in (147 cm × 198 cm). (Ulster Folk and Transport Museum)

Multi-coloured patchwork quilt, sewn with one-inch squares cut from uniform cloth of the Highland Light Infantry about 1880. The quilt, which is backed with printed cotton and edged with fringing, was made by Colour Sergeant R. Cumming while stationed at Maryhill Barracks, Glasgow. It was exhibited in the Royal Military Exhibition of 1890 at the Royal Hospital, Chelsea. 6 ft 2 in × 6 ft 6 in (188 cm × 198 cm). (Glasgow Museums and Art Galleries)

Corporal H. Trull of The Duke of Cambridge's Own (Middlesex Regiment) to report that the patchwork table cover he entered in the exhibition contained 15,500 pieces of cloth in fifteen different colours. Lance Sergeant J. Gardiner of the 2nd Battalion The Cheshire Regiment accomplished rather less – his table cloth contained 12,887 pieces of cloth.

Soldiers' quilts are generally without a filling and unquilted, the heaviness of the cloth making quilting almost impossible. Sometimes they are decorated with fringed borders and backed. The patchwork cover made by Colour Sergeant R. Cumming of The Highland Light Infantry (see page 114), in the same exhibition, was edged with fringing and backed with printed cotton. The Highland Light Infantry had a diversity of craft entries in the Chelsea exhibition, including paintings, a door-curtain of embroidery, an officer's oak bath tub and an inlaid chess table. Nor was

Sergeant Cumming, who also exhibited his fretwork brackets, the only regimental patchworker. The regiment also had a Private Pettigrew who had become fascinated by the challenge of piecing. Regrettably, the details of Private Pettigrews 'fancy patchwork bedrug' were unrecorded.

Sailors, who also had a facility with needle and thread, must also have sewn the occasional piece of patchwork, although this is less well documented. The one documented quilt made aboard ship was that made by Nicholas White of Dundee, who was a steward on two different whaling ships, the *Balaena* and *Terra Nova*. He obviously had access to books of cotton samples, especially those using the popular Turkey Red dyes (see page 49). His remarkable quilt contains over one hundred different prints, including about thirty-five varieties of stripes and line checks in twenty different colourways.

CHILDREN'S WORK

There is something very appealing about quilts made for or by children. Many were quite utilitarian in terms of fabric and design – often just squares of scraps hastily assembled. Others showed a bit of imaginative recycling and adaptation. Children's cloth books, for example, were usable for quilt piecing: the pages of one such illustrated alphabet book were assembled by one mother or grandmother to form the medallion of an otherwise utilitarian bed-cover.[13] And a quilt made for William Helyh Llewellyn of Bridgend, Glamorgan in 1856 (see page 116) also had a printed centre – with children on a seesaw.

Quilts that reveal the difficulties many young girls have in developing a facility with the needle have a special attraction. The delightful picture of a woman milking a green cow with pink polka dots, so laboriously stitched in canvas by young May Bowan in Wales at the beginning of this century, is a good example (see page 117). The canvas work provides a unique medallion centre for the surrounding 'brickwork' squares of tweed and wool. The squares, which are not square, have been feather-stitched in red and the quilting done in well-spaced waves.

The same naive quality is to be found in the work of Ann Clemishaw, who at nineteen years of age was considerably older than May but obviously still a learner. The crewel embroidery she used in her sample-piece medallion quilt in 1827 is almost primitive in style yet the sentiment of the verse is truly filial:

What's in Thy Mind Let No One Know
Not to Thy Friend Thy Secret Show

For if Thy Friend should Prove Thy Foe
Then Would All the World Thy Secret Know

This I have Done to Let You See
What care my Parents Took of Me

Ann Clemishaw Her Work
Osbaldwick Aged 19 years
in the Year of Our Lord 1827[14]

The use of sample pieces of embroidery or crewel work as the centre medallion of a quilt seemed to enjoy a certain popularity in the first half of the nineteenth century. A quilt at least offered a practical end to the many hours of often laborious sewing that went into the sample pieces. The remainder of the quilt, often as not, was paid little heed. The bed-cover made by Ann Clemishaw, for example, ended as a frame quilt, the large borders of uncoordinated furnishing fabric being added with haste and little thought. Roseanna Butler of County Antrim followed a similar course in 1844 when she surrounded her sample piece of wool embroidery with borders of dress fabric (see page 119).

It is assumed, from the crudity of the embroidery, that sample piece quilts were usually made by young women learning to use the needle for decorative as opposed to utilitarian purposes. The less ambitious and gifted no doubt heaved a long sigh of relief at being able to finish the centre panel of embroidery: others demonstrated more patience

115

Child's pieced quilt with printed centre of children on a seesaw. Made for
William Helyh Llewellyn (1849-1877) of Bridgend, Glamorgan, in 1856. 2 ft 9 in
× 3 ft 10 in (84 cm × 117 cm). (Photograph courtesy of the Welsh Folk Museum)

May Bowan of Wales stitched this primitive work in the early 1900s. The polka dot cow in the centre is canvas work and the surrounding squares of tweed and wool have been feather stitched in red. 4 ft 7 in × 5 ft 8 in (140 cm × 172 cm). (Ron Simpson)

Centre frame of Broderie Perse and pieced quilt made by Ann Thompson in 1824. The centre features a sampler verse in cross stitch, 'Early Will I Seek Thee', surrounded by Broderie Perse, framed by appliquéd hearts on pieced squares. The quilt is backed with linen and quilted in shells but has no filling. 8 ft × 8 ft 5 in (244 cm × 257 cm). (The Castle Museum, York)

Medallion quilt with wool embroidery surrounded by scrap borders. Signed
'Roseanna Butler 17 August 1844 Randalstown, Co. Antrim.' Wave quilted. 6 ft
6 in × 6 ft 7 in (198 cm × 201 cm). (Ulster Folk and Transport Museum)

and creativity and carried their decorative sewing abilities into the remainder of the quilt. It is not known how old Ann Thompson was in 1824 when she made her quilt (see page 118) but she demonstrated an ability to use Broderie Perse, appliqué and quilting as well as fine cross stitch. The sampler verse she worked – 'Early Will I Seek Thee' – has frames of dress cottons, applied red hearts and a wreath of flowers cut from printed fabric.

Surviving examples of such youthful industry are rare. Undertaking the piecing or quilting for a complete bed-cover would have been a daunting task for most young children, which is probably why most of the patchwork done by children was restricted to small items like pin-cushions or bags. Inevitably, however, the question arises as to whether patchwork was ever taught as a specific technique in the nineteenth century – at a period when so much emphasis was put on practical and decorative needle skill.

Needlework sample books, dated 1826, from the Farnham Model School, County Monaghan, are in the collection of the Ulster Folk and Transport Museum. Among the tiny garments which pupils were required to sew to prove their ability at turning heels, making shirts and the like, are patchwork hexagon flowers. The indications are, however, that these shapes were then used to teach the elements of oversewing, just as squares were used for fine hemming or practising buttonholing. Oversewing is, of course, the technique used when patchwork is assembled with paper templates. Some forty years later, the teaching emphasis had changed from pure sewing technique to possible projects. In *The Manual of Needlework*, a teachers' guide published by the Kildare Place Society in Dublin in 1869, the same hexagon flower appears again. In this instance, however, the hexagon is presented as an alternative to working with the square and the making of quilts is suggested – with directions which would undoubtedly surprise some modern day quiltmakers.

In the classroom, different stages of quilt piecing were apparently handled by pupils of varying abilities. Squares were first hemmed by a beginning class and then handed over to the next class up, to be sewn together in groups of four to form a diamond of two printed and two white squares 'placed angularly'. Thus were two sewing techniques taught – hemming and seaming. The obvious way to make practical use of this youthful enterprise was to put the squares together as a quilt – not, however, before these units had been 'lined separately, and the edges of the lining turned in on every side'. Thus 'a very substantial quilt can be made up and lined at the same time, and a large supply of work for practice be furnished to a school.' These lined squares had no wadding but were required to be quilted individually before being joined, a stage which, the teacher was advised, could 'be done by either of the two next higher classes'.

The attractions of patchwork were undoubtedly communicated by sources outside the school. For the poorer families, basic sewing skills were a necessity and the piecing of utilitarian quilts so ordinary as to go unrecorded. The girls of wealthier families would learn the rudiments of ornamental sewing and, depending on their individual artistic bent, take it from there. Or perhaps they would derive inspiration from publications like *How to Make Common Things*.

The editor of this volume was Charles Peters, editor of *The Girl's Own Indoor Book,* and the chapter entitled 'A Chat About Quilts and Patchwork' begins: 'The rage for eccentricities may be carried to the extreme, but the play of fancy, with proper regard to art and beauty, is both commendable and improving.'

These opening remarks conclude with: '. . . for it is pleasant for the eye to be gratified with pictures of beauty which those possessed of wealth can, and do, produce.'[15]

Patchwork, according to the editor, had become somewhat old-fashioned in the light of crewel and art needlework but he had high praise for its advantages:

[It] is so useful an assistant in teaching children to work, in giving instruction in neatness and deftness of fingering, that it has always, and will always, keep its place in the course of tuition in schools for plain needlework.[16]

Suggestions for making quilts included 'rich satin quilts in squares of different colours, each square embroidered in bouquets or foreign birds in all their rich shades . . . and joined together by fancy stitches in fine gold thread.' Alternative ideas were a less expensive covering in stripes of *guipure d'art* and bands of broad satin ribbon, either plain, painted or embroidered, the quilt being edged in lace; or cretonne work on satin cloth or twilled cotton, with edges scalloped with washable crewels.

For pieced quilts, the young readers were recommended to try the 'chessboard pattern' described as 'probably the oldest pattern in patchwork . . . the arrangement of simple squares of various colours with white in alternation.' Instruction concentrated on the method of sewing with papers and quilting: 'all the counterpanes need wadding and quilting, the latter being merely running it all over in a set pattern or in simple straight lines crossing each other, and so forming diamonds and squares. It can also be done by a sewing machine.'

By the turn of the century we find publications like *The Girl's Sewing Book*, edited by Flora Klickmann (circa 1900). This publication 'From the Office of the Girl's Own Paper and Woman's Magazine', gave directions for making a patchwork quilt for a doll's bed. In this instance the directions also were for sewing with papers (cut from stiff paper like old letters) and arranging the squares alternately in dark and light. Due regard was given to the finishing: the instructions called for mitred corners in the unbleached calico border and an embroidered chevron stitch around the edge.

Although the followers of the Arts and Crafts Movement in the late nineteenth and early twentieth centuries were not quiltmakers (though they did make appliquéd coverlets) in the manner of their Victorian predecessors, their teaching concepts in sewing showed a complete swing away from the kind of regimented or disciplined instruction that had previously been followed. The simplicity they advocated was a reaction to the fussy ornamentation of the Victorian era, and although both relied on appliqué as a technique, the materials they used changed dramatically – silks and velvets for the one, plain woven linens for the other. Also, in teaching there was less emphasis on stitchery perfection and more on artistic development.

Educational Needlecraft, the book written by Margaret Swanson and Ann Macbeth, both instructresses at the Glasgow School of Art during its Mackintosh renaissance, is an important record, showing how young needlewomen were being influenced at the beginning of the century. Ann Macbeth believed that children had an inborn creativity and that they should be allowed to express their imagination without hindrance. Sewing was not to be taught in such a way that it became a dreaded task, rather it was meant to stimulate creative power. The book has lessons intended for children from the age of six, right up to the experienced practitioner at the age of twenty-four, and opens with some fundamental guidelines:

The underlying idea in all education is development of intelligence and formation of character.

   Towards this end, the training of the hand and the eye has to be reckoned with. One method of instruction lies through that ancient and cheap tool – the needle – which gives the *Form* of stitchery; and through material, which gives the *Colour* used in construction and decoration. Which become one by means of *Art*.[17]

Much emphasis was placed on the development of eyesight in connection with sewing, the authors stating that only at the age of eleven, when a child's eyesight had achieved 'normal vision', could they be asked to use white thread on a white ground. Between the ages of six and eleven years the child had a sense of form which was large and a sense of colour which was bright. The skill for handwork was not achieved until between the ages of eleven and twelve, at which time it needed to be 'seized at once and properly directed'. The necessity for freedom to experiment was also espoused – the 'graciousness of Art . . . Beauty must come back to the useful arts, and the distinction between the fine and the useful arts be forgotten'.[18]

Sewing is a craft with a long and vigorous history in Britain and any examination of quiltmaking has to be made within that tradition. Quilts were made and used at every level of society – for the miner's cottage, the middle-class home, aristocratic mansion and royal castle. Sometimes they were made for pleasure and sometimes out of economic necessity. Whatever the reason, antique quilts are best appreciated by a knowledge of the circumstances which dictated their creation.

Those admirers of British quilt treasures who can look beyond the faded cotton patch and the irregular stitch will discover a craft filled with romance – a romance that not only enriches the pages of British history but also stretches across the oceans to touch the lands of the Commonwealth and the United States.

Notes

   1. Appliquéd and pieced linen bed-cover in the collection of the Gunnersbury Park Museum, London, circa 1810.
   2. The collection of Liverpool Museums.
   3. Daniel Rock, *Textile Fabrics*, London, 1876, p.108.
   4. S.F.A. Caulfield, *The Dictionary of Needlework*, London, 1887, p.414.
   5. Dora de Blaquiere et al., *How to Make Common Things: A Handy Book for Girls*, London, 1890.
   6. Ibid., p.36.
   7. Ibid., p.38. ('Berlin' patterns refers to designs usually worked in wool on canvas.)
   8. The collection of Leicestershire Museums.
   9. The collection of the National Museums of Scotland.
   10. John Cunningham, *The Quakers*, London, 1867.
   11. Katharine Fry and Mrs Rachel E. Cresswell (eds), *Memoirs of the Life of Elizabeth Fry*, London: John Hatch and Son, 1848, p.265.
   12. Ibid., p.429.
   13. The collection of the Ulster Folk and Transport Museum.
   14. The collection of the Castle Museum, York.
   15. de Blaquiere et al., op cit.
   16. Ibid., p.31.
   17. Margaret Swanson and Ann Macbeth, *Educational Needlecraft*, London, 1911, p.1.
   18. Ibid., p.3.

Select Bibliography

Alford, Lady Marian. *Needlework as Art.* London: Sampson Low, 1886.

Callen, Anthea. *Women in the Arts and Crafts Movement 1870–1914.* London: Astragal Books, 1979.

Caulfield, S.F.A. and Blanche C. Saward. *The Dictionary of Needlework.* London: L. Upcott Gill, 1887.

Colby, Averil. *Patchwork.* London: Batsford, 1958.

Colby, Averil. *Quilting.* London: Batsford, 1972.

Day, Lewis F. and Mary Buckle. *Art in Needlework.* London: Batsford, 1900.

de Blaquiere, Dora, Marie Karger et al. *How to Make Common Things: A Handy Book for Girls.* London: The Religious Tract Society, 1890.

de Dillmont, Therese. *Needlework and Embroidery.* Germany, 1886. Reprinted (ed. Mary Gostelow), Dorset: Alpha Books, 1982.

Digby, George W. *Elizabethan Embroidery.* London: Faber and Faber, 1963.

Dorinda, *Needlework for Ladies for Pleasure and Profit.* London: W. Swan Sonnenschein, 1883.

Field, June. *Collecting Georgian and Victorian Crafts.* London: Heinemann, 1973.

Finch, Karen and Greta Putnam. *The Care and Preservation of Textiles.* London: Batsford, 1985.

Fitzrandolph, Mavis. *Traditional Quilting.* London: Batsford, 1954.

Gifford, M.K. *Needlework* (The Hobby Books). London: Thomas Nelson, n.d.

Glaister, Elizabeth. *Needlework.* London: Macmillan, 1880.

Grant, I.F. *Highland Folk Ways.* London: Routledge and Kegan Paul, 1961.

Hake, Elizabeth. *English Quilting Old and New.* London: Batsford, 1937.

Hughes, Therle. *English Domestic Needlework 1660–1860.* London: Lutterworth Press, 1961.

Irwin, John and Katharine Brett. *Origins of Chintz.* London: HMSO, 1970.

Jones, Mary Eirwen. *Welsh Crafts.* London: Batsford, 1978.

Kendrick, A.F. *English Needlework.* (1933) Second edition (rev. Patricia Wardle), London: A. and C. Black, 1967.

Lethaby, W.R. *Home and Country Arts.* Compilation of articles reprinted from *Home and Country,* the NFWI Magazine, London, 1923.

Levey, Santina M. *Discovering Embroidery of the 19th Century.* Aylesbury, Bucks: Shire Publications, 1977.

Lewis, Frank. *English Chintz.* Leigh-on-Sea: F. Lewis, 1935.

Lichten, Frances. *Decorative Art of Victoria's Era.* London: Charles Scribner, 1950.

Lockwood, M.S. and E. Glaister. *Art Embroidery.* London: Marcus Ward, 1878.

McKendry, Ruth. *Quilts and Other Bed Coverings in the Canadian Tradition.* Toronto: Von Nostrand Reinhold, 1979.

Manual of Needlework. Dublin: Kildare Place Society, 1869.

Masters, Ellen T. *The Gentlewoman's Book of Art Needlework.* London: Henry and Co., 1893.

Meldrum, Alex. *Irish Patchwork.* Dublin: Kilbenny Design Workshops, 1979.

Minter, David C. (ed.). *Modern Needlecraft.* London: Blackie, 1933.

Morris, Barbara. *Victorian Embroidery.* London: Herbert Jenkins, 1962.

Morris, May. *Decorative Needlework.* London: Joseph Hughes, 1893.

Mulliner, H.H. *The Decorative Arts in England 1660–1780.* London: Batsford, 1924.

Robinson, Stuart. *A History of Printed Textiles.* London: Studio Vista, 1969.

Robinson, Stuart. *A History of Dyed Textiles.* London: Studio Vista, 1969.

Rock, Daniel. *Textile Fabrics.* London: Chapman and Hall, 1876.

Scott, B. *The Craft of Quilting.* Leicester: Dryad, 1928.

Shaw-Smith, David. *Ireland's Traditional Crafts.* London: Thames and Hudson, 1984.

Snook, Barbara. *English Embroidery.* London: Bell and Hyman, 1985.

Swain, Margaret H. *Historical Needlework*. London: Barrie and Jenkins, 1970.

Swain, Margaret H. *Figures on Fabric*. London: A. and C. Black, 1980.

Swain, Margaret H. *Scottish Embroidery*. London: Batsford, 1986.

Swanson, Margaret and Ann Macbeth. *Educational Needlecraft*. London: Longmans, Green, 1911.

Symonds, Mary (Mrs Guy Antrobus) and Louisa Preece. *Needlework Through the Ages*. London: Hodder and Stoughton, 1928.

Synge, Lanto. *Antique Needlework*. Dorset: Blandford, 1982.

Thomas, Mary. *Embroidery Book*. London: Hodder and Stoughton, 1936.

Tozer, Jane and Sarah Levitt. *Fabric of Society*. Powys: Laura Ashley, 1983.

Valentine, Mrs L.J. (ed.). *The Girl's Home Companion*. London: Frederick Warner, 1906.

Warren, Geoffrey. *A Stitch in Time*. Newton Abbot, Devon: David and Charles, 1976.

Webster, Marie D. *Quilts: Their Story and How to Make Them*. London: Batsford, 1915.

Weldon's Encyclopaedia of Needlework. London, 1939.

Whitley, Mrs Mary (ed.). *Every Girl's Book of Sport, Occupation and Pastime*. London: George Routledge and Son, 1897.

Wilton, Countess of. *The Art of Needlework*. London: Henry Colburn, 1840.

Articles, Periodicals and Catalogues

Anthony, Ilid E., 'Quilting and Patchwork in Wales', *Amgueddfa* (Bulletin of the National Museum of Wales), No. 12, Winter 1972.

Bowes Museum, *North Country Quilting*. Exhibition Catalogue, 1963.

Emerson, Mrs Rose, 'Quilting', *Journal of the Glens of Antrim Historical Society*, Vol. 4, 1976.

Garrad, Larch S., 'Quilting and Patchwork in the Isle of Man', *Folk Life*, Vol. 17, 1979.

Glasgow School of Art, Catalogue, Exhibition of Ancient & Modern Embroidery and Needlecraft, 1916.

Great Exhibition of 1851, Catalogue, London.

Harris, Katherine, 'Patchwork and Appliqué Bed Covers', *Ulster Folk Museum Yearbook*, 1966-7.

Hay, M. Doriel, 'Traditional Quilting in England and Wales', *The Embroideress*, 1925.

Jones, Laura, 'Quilting', *Ulster Folk Life*, Vol. 21, 1975.

Jones, Laura, 'Patchwork Bedcovers', *Ulster Folk Life*, Vol. 24, 1978.

Macfarlane, Fiona and Elizabeth Arthur, *Glasgow School of Art Embroidery 1894–1920*. Exhibition Catalogue, Glasgow Museums and Art Galleries, 1980.

MacGregor, Gylla MacGregor of, 'Notes on the SWRI National Exhibition of Needlework', *Scottish Home and Country*, September 1934.

Morton, Deirdre E., 'Quilting in Glenlark, Co. Tyrone', *Ulster Folk Life*, Vol. 5, 1959.

Museum of Science and Art, Edinburgh. Catalogue of Loan Collection of Art Needlework, 1877.

Needle & Thread, III. July 1914. (ed. Mrs Archibald Christie).

Peel, R.A., 'Turkey Red Dyeing in Scotland', *The Journal of the Society of Dyers & Colourists*, Vol. 68, 1952.

Royal Military Exhibition 1890 (Royal Hospital, Chelsea), Catalogue, 1890.

Saward, B.C., 'Needlework Suggestions', *The Housewife*, Vol. 3, 1888.

Scottish Women's Rural Institutes. Catalogue of National Exhibition of Needlework, Edinburgh, 1934.

Sylvia's Home Journal, 1883–92.

Tyne & Wear County Council Museums Service, Information Sheets on Quilts, n.d.

Victoria and Albert Museum, *Notes on Applied Work and Patchwork*, 1949.

Ward, Anne, 'Quilting in the North of England', *Folk Life*, Vol. 4, 1966.

Weldon's Practical Needlework series, 1881–92.

Index

Numbers in italics refer to illustrations